PHENOMENOLOGY OF INTUITION AND EXPRESSION

Also available from *Continuum*:

Essence of Human Freedom, Martin Heidegger
Essence of Truth, Martin Heidegger
Mindfulness, Martin Heidegger
Towards the Definition of Philosophy

Forthcoming:

Basic Problems of Phenomenology, Martin Heidegger
The Concept of Time, Martin Heidegger

MARTIN HEIDEGGER
PHENOMENOLOGY OF INTUITION AND EXPRESSION
Theory of Philosophical Concept Formation

Translated by Tracy Colony

continuum

Continuum International Publishing Group
The Tower Building
11 York Road
London SE1 7NX

80 Maiden Lane
Suite 704
New York NY 10038

www.continuumbooks.com

This English translation © Continuum 2010

The translation of this work was supported by a grant from the Goethe-Institut which is funded by the German Ministry of Foreign Affairs

Originally published in German as *Phänomenologie der Anschauung und des Ausdrucks*
© Vittorio Klostermann GmbH, Frankfurt am Main, 1993

All rights reserved. No part of this publication may be reproduced or transmitted in any form or by any means, electronic or mechanical, including photocopying, recording, or any information storage or retrieval system, without prior permission in writing from the publishers.

British Library Cataloguing-in-Publication Data
A catalogue record for this book is available from the British Library

ISBN: HB: 978-1-8470-6443-1
　　　PB: 978-1-8470-6444-8

Library of Congress Cataloguing-in-Publication Data
Heidegger, Martin, 1889–1976.
　　[Phänomenologie der Anschauung und des Ausdrucks. English]
　　Phenomenology of intuition and expression/Martin Heidegger; translated by Tracy Colony.
　　　p. cm.
　　Includes bibliographical references (p.).
　　ISBN 978-1-84706-443-1 – ISBN 978-1-84706-444-8
　1. Philosophy. I. Title.

　　B3279.H48P4313 2010
　　193–dc22

2009047106

Typeset by BookEns, Royston, Herts.

Contents

Translator's foreword   xi

Introduction: the problem situation of philosophy   1
§ 1 The function of a 'Theory of Philosophical Concept Formation' in phenomenology   1
§ 2 The distinction between scientific philosophy and worldview philosophy   6
§ 3 Life philosophy and culture philosophy – the two main groups of contemporary philosophy   8
§ 4 Life as primal phenomenon and the two problem groups of contemporary philosophy   12
    (a) Life as objectifying and the problem of absolute validity (the problem of the a priori)   13
    (b) Life as experiencing and the problem of the irrational (the problem of lived experience)   17
§ 5 The phenomenological destruction   21
    (a) The function of phenomenology within the whole of philosophizing   21
    (b) The boundedness of phenomenological destruction to preconception   24
    (c) Philosophy and factical life experience   26

CONTENTS

  (d) The application of the destruction in the two problem groups   28

PART ONE   31

On the destruction of the problem of the a priori   33
§ 6 The six meanings of history and first bringing-out of the pre-delineations in them   33
§ 7 The right pursuit of the pre-delineations: the explication of the sense-complexes   38
§ 8 Characterization of relation: the articulation of the sense-complexes according to the sense of relation   46
§ 9 The role of the historical within the a priori tendency of philosophy   51
§ 10 Characterization of enactment: the articulation of the sense-complexes according to the sense of enactment   56
  (a) The task of phenomenological dijudication   56
  (b) The phenomenological dijudication of the genuine enactments of the meaning-complexes in question   57

PART TWO   67

On the destruction of the problem of lived experience   69
§ 11 The transition to the second problem group and the relation between psychology and philosophy   69

Section One
The destructing consideration of the Natorpian position   73
§ 12 The four viewpoints of destruction   73
§ 13 Natorp's general reconstructive psychology   77
  (a) The method of reconstruction   77
  (b) The disposition of psychology   83
§ 14 The carrying-out of the destruction   87
  (a) In which tendency does Natorp approach the complex of lived experience?   87
  (b) Which is the character of unity and manifoldness of the complex of lived experience?   90
  (c) How does the 'I' comport itself in the complex of lived experience?   95
  (d) How is the 'I' itself had?   95

§ 15 Constitution as guiding preconception	99
a) The primacy of the method	99
b) The determination of the problem of the 'I' through the idea of constitution	101
c) The radicalization of the theoretical in the idea of constitution	106
d) Enactmental and order-complex	113

Section Two
The destructing consideration of the Diltheyian position   115
§ 16 The attitudinal character of Natorp's philosophy and the
     expectation of the opposite in Dilthey's   115
§ 17 Report on Dilthey's philosophy   120
§ 18 The destruction of the Diltheyian philosophy   125
§ 19 Natorp and Dilthey – the task of philosophy   129

Appendix   135
Editor's afterword to the second edition   155
Glossary   159
Notes   161
Index   167

For the philosophers use words in whatever way they like, and they do not bother to avoid offending the ears of religious men even in the most difficult matters. But we are obliged by religious duty to speak according to a fixed rule, lest verbal licence beget impious opinions concerning the matters which our words signify.
Augustine, *The City of God*, X, 23

The interior man puts the care of himself before all other concerns.
Thomas à Kempis, *The Imitation of Christ*, II, 5

Translator's foreword

This book is a translation of *Phänomenologie der Anschauung und des Ausdrucks: Theorie der Philosophischen Begriffsbildung*, first published in 1993 as Volume 59 of Martin Heidegger's *Gesamtausgabe*. This translation is based on the slightly revised 2007 edition of this volume. The text is derived from the manuscript of a lecture course which Heidegger delivered at Freiburg University in the summer semester of 1920. The final sections of this manuscript are lost. In place of these missing sections a transcript by Oskar Becker has been inserted by the German editor. More details about the origin and compilation of the text are given in the Editor's afterword.

Heidegger never intended or prepared this manuscript for publication. Accordingly, many of its passages have the rough yet condensed and rich character of notes prepared to support further elaboration. In translating this text, I have not attempted to moderate this characteristic of Heidegger's composition. At the same time, I have striven, as much as possible, for a clear and readable translation. I have also endeavoured to maintain consistency regarding the many words that Heidegger clearly employs as technical terms. I have rendered them consistently throughout and have included them in the appended English–German glossary. With respect to terminological consistency, wherever possible I have tried to maintain continuity with other English language translations of Heidegger from this period. As is now standard in translations of Heidegger, I have also chosen to leave the term *Dasein* most often untranslated and unitalicized. Where the word *Dasein* is employed in a clearly prosaic sense, I have rendered it as 'existence'.

TRANSLATOR'S FOREWORD

One particular translation challenge that this text presents is Heidegger's use of the terms *Gehalt* and *Inhalt*, which are both customarily translated by the word 'content'. Whereas Heidegger often chooses to employ the term *Gehalt* to designate a more originary sense of content, in contrast to the more inertial sense of content as *Inhalt*, this difference is usually clear from the context, so I have chosen not to complicate the text at this level by introducing a new term.

When I felt it necessary to indicate that the translation fails to reflect an important aspect or nuance of Heidegger's text, I have interpolated the original German in square brackets. Heidegger's references to other works are translated in the text and given in their original versions in the Notes. There are no translator's notes.

For invaluable criticisms and sagacious advice, I would like to express my gratitude to Theodore Kisiel. For meticulous and faithful assistance in the preparation of this translation, I would like to deeply thank Maren Mittentzwey.

Tracy Colony
September 2009

Introduction: the problem situation of philosophy

§ 1 The function of a 'Theory of Philosophical Concept Formation' in phenomenology

The theme gives the impression of being a special problem and strikes one as a conscious concession to the specialization that today is fashionably much resisted. The next given reading would then lie in the opinion that it concerns specifically aesthetic problems, even with a particular relationship to expressionist art. The perplexity would only apparently be alleviated if I were to try to 'explain' right at the beginning the meaning of the words 'phenomenology', 'intuition' and 'expression' one after the other. That would lead to certain propositions and determinations that would merely create the illusion of guaranteeing a genuine understanding. At best, just sticking to words could be further encouraged. That this is not at all the way in which philosophy works is exactly what shall also be shown in these considerations. And yet, leaving aside fixed definitions, there are ways to lead towards the point of the question. To carry this out in a concrete way that would also take into account philosophy's questions regarding principles is the preliminary and only goal of the following deliberations.

The subtitle 'Theory of Philosophical Concept Formation' indicates that the task is nevertheless aiming at something fundamental, although one cannot help suspecting that even in this way it still concerns a more remote task, which, on top of that and especially nowadays, has to confront a particularly acute opposition. Provided that it is the intention

THE PROBLEM SITUATION OF PHILOSOPHY

to lead step by step out of the contemporary philosophical situation as a whole and, along the guidelines of its typical configurations of problems, into the complex of problems, it becomes necessary to first of all indicate the resistances encountered in a first rough approach to the sought problem.

At first, one might consider such a theory of philosophical concept formation as abundantly premature, judging from the plausible relationship that every theory of that kind apparently must have to philosophy itself. A philosophy must have first achieved a certain level of conceptual-thematic development and systematic completion in order to allow, as it were, the structure of its concepts and the method of concept formation to be read off.

Provided that we are, however, of the conviction that we are really philosophizing and that means always working on a reshaping [*Neugestaltung*] of philosophy, it must also be simultaneously granted that the concrete structural complex of philosophy, in the fully sufficient totality of its fundamental features, is not remotely achieved and that therefore the theory of concept formation necessarily related to it cannot yet be undertaken at all.

The unambiguous factum of philosophy in concrete configuration is the precondition for a possible research into its structure. This necessary dependence of all so-directed structural research on the respective preceding and factical being-available of the concretion of science can be shown in Kantian philosophy and its 'gaps' which are much belaboured again today and have been for the last half century. The system of Kantian philosophy is lacking, so one says, for one thing the systematic setting-out – analogous to the critique of the knowledge of nature – of the a priori transcendental conditions of possibility of the human sciences, especially the science of history; in Kant's time there were no developed historical human sciences. Likewise, a primordial, pure research into the independent a priori of religion is lacking because Kant did not recognize the latter as a primordial phenomenon, but rather included it in morality.

However, with respect to philosophy itself and the task of a consideration pertaining to the theory of science and directed back to philosophy itself, one would nevertheless like to find a way out. Because even if a theory related to the tendencies, approaches and initial ground-laying creations would necessarily have to reach into what is vacillating and flowing, one could still try to make it possibly understandable by referring to the history of philosophy. The latter's abundance in concrete immortal achievements is undisputable even with the restriction to the philosophers of first and undisputed rank, especially for a philosophy that presses away from an epigonic mere adoption of standpoints and systems from history and pushes towards radical questioning. Exactly in this wanting-to-become-free from an un-genuine, non-primordially appropriated tradition this philosophy is always obligated to the continuing existence of what it 'deconstructs' [*abbaut*], not fortuitously but for primordially philosophical reasons.

But the historical past – the creations of philosophy, however readily the works seem to be accessible still today – is no erratic block that one encounters as standing there steadfast and complete and that one can confidently scan from all sides. The past of intellectual history only becomes objective in living understanding. The historical philosophies as facta are objective only in living philosophical apprehension. The past newly grows towards every living present in a particular way and within certain limits. The fundamental sense of intellectual history – and every history – is pre-delineated [*vorgezeichnet*] by the living preconception that leads and guides understanding.

But it would after all – renouncing for a moment an independent posing of problems – be possible, by closely following the Kantian or Hegelian philosophy, to unitarily interpret the history of philosophy from there and in this way make available a sufficiently abundant concrete material of factical philosophy that would also be free from the disadvantage of the isolating restriction to a single system. This material could serve as the basis for a theory of philosophical concept formation. The certainly limited fruitfulness of such an attempt should not be simply rejected here.

However, is not – granted, in every respect, the feasibility of such a theory related to the entire unitarily interpreted history of philosophy as factum – the very idea of such a theory already something secondary and essentially belated, indeed superfluous and uncreative? Is this idea not the suspicious sign of a mechanized excess of reflection, a philosophizing about philosophy? This objection is certainly apt in principle; it already characterizes the idea of the task – to say nothing of its factical realization – as exposed to weighty reservations.

(The first conscious attempt at a 'logic of philosophy' on the basis of a transcendental philosophy of value was made by Lask, without getting any further than programmatic intimations. His early death as a soldier brought these plans to naught.)

THE PROBLEM SITUATION OF PHILOSOPHY

The above objection bears on such an attempt all the more decisively, when the latter is to be set in motion within the tendency towards a reshaping of philosophy so that such a theory would amount to a premature hyper-reflective blocking-off of every positive problematic built 'on the matters themselves'. This objection is inescapable. The questionability of such a theory is complete as long as one sees the problem simply within the framework of a specifically transcendental-critical or transcendental-dialectical philosophy of reflection. Here there is the difficulty of the factum that is to be presupposed and here, on the standpoint of reflection, and only here, there is a new potential excess towards hyper-reflection and its secondary, fruitless 'results'.

It is therefore necessary to step completely out of this framework and come into the open [*ins Freie*]. With that the mentioned difficulties may fall away, but for that the uncertainties of a tendency towards reshaping are inhibiting. The phenomenological basic posture, provided that one understands it in the widest sense as descriptive analysis of the essence of the phenomena of consciousness that are not psychologically apperceived, is, however, not sufficient for a fundamental philosophical problematic as long as it is not itself genuinely philosophically primordially explicated. Critical advancements can certainly already be made from the basic posture alone; the edifice of an entire philosophy can be broken apart and shaken in its individual linkages; it is also possible to perform, within a limited region, positive, epistemic work in terms of subject matter. But if the ultimate – I do not say the 'systematic' – sense-relations that converge in a concrete concept of phenomenological philosophy that organically grows out of the sense of the phenomenological basic posture are missing, then the problems do not come to a full resolution and the perspectives of positive philosophizing itself remain concealed. At the same time, the danger of lapsing into a given but now purified and radicalized philosophical standpoint constantly persists, i.e. the danger of falling back into the commonly accepted framework of the philosophical problematic.

The goal of our concrete task is exactly to attain the idea as well as the concept and basic structure of phenomenological philosophy as co-motivated out of the phenomenological basic posture and to therewith for its part 'concept'-ualize that posture itself. That means: The *theory of philosophical concept formation* has in phenomenology itself a completely different position than in the philosophy of reflection. It is therefore not the correlate of a reflection externally imposed on a complete philosophy,

THEORY OF PHILOSOPHICAL CONCEPT FORMATION

but the enactmental and existing effectuation of philosophy itself. That which is sought has to be one of the radical problems if with its solution a getting at the sense of phenomenological philosophy is to be possible. This explicating and determining of the essence of philosophy may not be further understood as a task of gaining knowledge, as the setting-out of a material content in itself, but must be understood enactmentally.

After all, it is at first not very clear that the problem of concept formation in the formulated form of a phenomenology of intuition and expression can have such a central meaning, even if one entirely takes distance from the hitherto familiar and cultivated form of its treatment. If one, however, poses the problem within the act of aiming at a radical new foundation of philosophy, then one must nevertheless pose oneself the following questions: First, whether the concept has a central position in philosophy; and then quite in principle, whether it makes sense at all to speak of concepts in philosophy; furthermore, whether concepts in the most commonly understood sense mean something remote from philosophy, whether they constitute the basic structure of the objecthood of philosophy or whether they can even affect it at all and, if so, in which sense.

Only in the direction of these questions is the subtitle to be comprehended. It is supposed to indicate that it concerns the element which the sciences know as 'concept', without hereby prejudging that the sense of 'scientific concept' is, according to its sense, something primordial. *Theory of Philosophical Concept Formation* is therefore a formula in the prevailing language of contemporary philosophy that is supposed to merely indicate something to be primordially understood. The decision about the sense, character and function of the 'philosophical concept' becomes dependent on how philosophizing itself, in opposition to the scientific-theoretical attitude towards subject matter, is determined according to origin and not according to classes.

This determination and the understanding of the manner of its enactment shall now be methodologically prepared, namely in such a way that from the distinctly comprehended present problem situation, with the tendency of leading towards the origin, the prevailing problematic is demonstrated as not primordial and the origin itself is in this way indicated as negative for the understanding.

THE PROBLEM SITUATION OF PHILOSOPHY

§ 2 The distinction between scientific philosophy and worldview philosophy

Every attempt at a radical 'laying of the ground' of philosophy – and in earnest, philosophy always remains with the giving of the ground, the calling attention to the ground – mostly presses in some form towards securing philosophy as absolute knowledge, as last and first science, and towards pre-delineating the guidelines and framework for subsequent work. In this way, the idea of *philosophy as strict science* also arose from phenomenological research. That meant, within the situation of intellectual history in which phenomenology had its breakthrough, a demarcation from other philosophical basic goals subsumed under the title of *worldview philosophy*.

With this division between strict scientific philosophy and worldview philosophy, the possibility, justification and necessity of concrete worldview formation in factical life, with its factical spiritual-mental difficulties, was in no way contested. Just as little was scientific philosophy's enquiring work towards knowledge barred from utilization for concrete spiritual life. On the contrary, exactly through it a genuine foundation of total spiritual life and being was to be worked out; although in the posture of strictly and constantly developing research that grows from generation to generation, that is patient and contents itself with its respective concrete goal and does not allow itself, 'on the basis of emotional needs', to be led astray into a premature bending-around of the problematic and to rash rounding-off conclusions and systems. Whether this idea of philosophy as strict science, in this form, is necessary and fully motivated in the idea of the phenomenological basic posture, must remain open at this point. For the time being it is important that the tension between 'scientific philosophy' and 'worldview philosophy' is understood as such.

We begin with a brief clarification of the phenomenon of 'worldview'. It is a figuration that, according to its sense of content, of relation and of enactment belongs entirely in the basic structure of factical life experience. If we understand every single and communal life in its totality as having grown out of *one* spiritual situation and maintaining and completing itself in it, then worldview means the living concrete motivation-complex of the fundamental stances, decisions and life-worlds that pervade the situation of *one* life. Worldview grows and falls to concrete life out of and within factical life experience; it is no theoretically discovered, no theoretically appropriated life and also no theoretically established figuration of some inter-subjective or supra-historical objecthood. Therefore, provided that one speaks of *one* worldview of some figure, community, generation or time, concrete life is conceptualized and objectified in a way that, up to now, is not yet philosophically clarified. (Cf. the contribution by Karl Jaspers, *Psychology of Worldviews*, which is really fundamentally and conceptually insufficient.)

Now, worldview philosophy can mean several things: first the exploratory shaping and inter-subjectively (with-worldly) making-available elaborating of such a worldview, whereas the sense of relation and of enactment of this kind of spiritual achievement – whether science, philosophy, poetry or all these in one – remains for the most part undetermined. The shaping and elaborating of a worldview is motivated from a situation of intellectual history. Worldview anticipates time and guides it; by concretely sweeping time along, it concurrently directs it. Worldview philosophy can mean furthermore: the relationally and enactmentally theoretically scientific exhibiting of the so-called supra-temporal basic goals and values of life from time and history and then equally a preparing of these goals and values for the concrete necessities of a spiritual present. Finally, the word can also mean the profession [*Bekenntnis*] of a person from its spiritual position in its time.

All three forms do not exclude strict scientific work; they will rather always require it and claim it for themselves – now implicitly, now with expressly methodological emphasis. Thus one was then able to say: The separation between scientific philosophy and worldview philosophy can be easily overcome in a scientific worldview philosophy, which neither gives a merely personal, contingent view of the world and life nor remains with the individual examinations based on results of knowledge and their propagation, without ultimate decisive horizons, which fundamentally is no philosophy at all.[1]

We will later see that this is a compromise, and must be one, because the division between strict scientific philosophy and worldview philosophy or – as Jaspers says in his *Psychology of Worldviews* – between merely scientifically *observing* philosophy and *prophetic* philosophy is itself not fully clarified and not radical, simply because of the fact that it is not asked whether the two phenomena 'science' and 'worldview' may at all be primarily linked to the idea of philosophy. It will thus turn out: The division is not to be rejected because it can actually be bridged, but because it may not be made at all and is, at its root, un-genuine; in other words, because it is 'enacted' in a dimension that, contrary to the primordial, the dimension in which philosophy explicates itself, is secondarily set apart and reified.

Both elements of the division conceal the access to the idea of phenomenological philosophy as long as one takes these as a fixed and not really problematic starting point for the question about the essence of philosophy. The formula of opposition *scientific philosophy – worldview philosophy* is the exponent of *the* structure of the philosophical problematic as it has dominated philosophy since Plato, although with certain interruptions. If the formula itself is to disappear as a non-primordial starting point for the problem, then the structure ultimately motivating it must first be brought into relief and then be destructed. The consideration restricts itself to the contemporary philosophical situation in which all decisive moments of the structure, as it were, are gathered together. This restriction is, in the context of the present task, permissible insofar as the aim is merely to first of all understand the problem. The radical explication of the phenomenological problematic whose sense is to be attained will know how to handle Greek philosophy (Plato and Aristotle) and equally modern philosophy since Descartes in the destructive aspect, such that only therewith the positively decisive destruction of Christian philosophy and theology clearly prepares itself.

§ 3 Life philosophy and culture philosophy – the two main groups of contemporary philosophy

The nowadays heavily emphasized, but not unambiguous attitudinal direction towards life-reality, life-advancement and life-intensification, as well as the now common and much cultivated talk about *life, life-feeling, lived experience* [*Erlebnis*] and *living experience* [*Erleben*] are the diversely motivated characteristics of our spiritual situation. It is not possible here to even briefly hint at the rich complex of motives, as it has developed from the Enlightenment, in its concretion. The moments shall be pointed out from which the problematic of present day philosophy is mainly determined.

What is decisive is the arousal of the pronounced awakening of an historical consciousness and its concrete experiential all-round elaboration in, on and from the historical human sciences. The Dasein-reality as becoming, developing, form-changing, self-differentiating life, which processes an ever richer abundance within itself, enters continuously further also into the determining content of factical life experience and allows for an ever clearer understanding of contemporary Dasein as a phase, level or transit point of a 'complete life'. The growing surge of life-forms [*Lebensgestalten*] of the most varied magnitude, the most varied style and the most varied strength, durability and tendency in one respect enriches Dasein, however, at the same time firmly holds it more in the direction of taking up, of comparative utilizing as well as of being stimulated and led. The present becomes 'historical' itself, in fact, not only in the sense of a phase of forward-pressing becoming, but also 'historical' in the sense that its basic contents are historically adopted and are actually no longer themselves created ones. As far as norm, goal and value questions appear in the different domains of life, norms and values are seen as *products* of a developmental thought and dissected as such. The disjointed elements are shown in their historical genesis and this *historical explanation* is at the same time regarded and brought into circulation as the subject matter [*sachliche*] decision about the questions.

This fundamental comprehension of all life-forms, realities and Dasein-elements as *products* of a development, the idealization of all decisive and ultimate validity of knowledge and science with the demonstration and proof of having-become from simple beginnings and elements was also reinforced and furthered through the development of biology, which simultaneously enacts itself along with the configuration of the historical human sciences. The extension of the biological notion of development to the human being and human organizations means the entry – or more exactly the formation of a new science – of sociology, which, for its part, lastingly determines the science of history. The formation of biology, above all of general physiology, brings along with it that of psychology, which initially enjoys extensive cultivation as physiological psychology, psychology of the sense organs, namely through the effect of ultimate natural-scientific, physical-mechanical principles on biology and psychology. Also here, genetic explanation became *the* form of scientific knowledge, also here it was attempted to build up mental-spiritual life out of ultimate simple elements. In this psychology, one strove at the same time for the most general human science as the basis of the science of history as well as of philosophy. Indeed, from both sides a strong opposition to this claim set in, which at once led to the idea of an understanding psychology [*verstehenden Psychologie*] and its development in Dilthey and at the same time to the research, as it pertains to the theory of science, into the structure of the human and cultural sciences. In philosophy, the pushing-away of natural-scientific psychology – on the basis of a renewal of Kantian philosophy – into different directions and from different motives meant a prevailing of the questions of the a priori, of the lawfulness of reason, of the ought, of validity, of values. This is accompanied by a stronger emphasis on the independence and autonomous lawfulness [*Eigengesetzlichkeit*] of spiritual life and by a stemming of the mechanistic notion of development, in psychology a no longer constrained by physiology research into 'higher mental life', in general the growing predominance of the psychology of lived experience.

The entwined cross-interacting of those motives and counter motives leads to the prevailing of the *spiritual* life reality and of life in general – the latter mainly determined from there and at the same time by biology. The problematic of contemporary philosophy is centered around life as *primal phenomenon*: It is either that life in general is posited as the primal phenomenon and all questions are directed back to this, that is, that every objecthood is comprehended as objectivation and manifestation *of* life – for example the philosophies of life as they, mainly in biological fundamental orientation, are connected to the names James and Bergson, in the fundamental orientation of the human sciences to the name of Dilthey and in one that also unifies both motive groups as well as the one that is to be mentioned in what follows, to the name of Simmel. Or life is seen as culture, as manifestation, but now with a view to the fact that this culture formation and life enacts itself and is supposed to enact itself in a bond to norm-giving principles and values. The goal of such consideration of life is then a universal a priori systematics of reason as it is strived for by the Marburg School, by Rickert and in the most recent development of his ideas by Husserl. In the basic aim, respectively, in the transcendental-philosophical basic orientation, an undeniable converging of the tendencies can be observed more clearly from year to year in those three directions: reason and value systematics as philosophy of culture. The way to this goal, the claims to ultimate foundation, the methodological means of the undertaking are certainly essentially different in the phenomenological systematics of reason than in the Marburg School and in Rickert.

The first group of philosophers is in part sharply opposed by the second, even if, by way of contrast, it must also be said that the second one has learned much from the first one. The second group is furthermore identified by the fact that in it the so-called logical-epistemological problematic plays an eminent and direction-giving role.

Oswald Spengler, who claims to give the last great philosophy of the Occident and presents its basic traits in the idea of a universal symbolics, gives – as far as the principal, fundamental, primarily decisive is concerned – merely an offshoot above all of the first mentioned group of motives of life philosophy, the one underpinned by an animated and oriented continuism. His philosophy is completely out of date and is largely obligated to the 'windy chatter' of the philosophies that he mentions, but even more of those philosophies he remains silent about. The notorious ignorance and journalistic superficiality of today's educated crowd had to seize on Spengler's book, especially since it has starkly positive and easily accessible but no philosophical qualities. But even competent people do not overcome the unclear discordancy of a now excessive admiration, now gruff repudiation, for even there what prevails is the inability to clearly see and take hold of what is fundamental and radical. This is now especially difficult in Spengler's case because the concrete details are extremely captivating and lead one to miss what is fundamental and even conceal it, thereby strengthening the proposed theory with the semblance of evidential power. The theory itself is nothing other than an especially emphatic compilation of the already mentioned motives of life philosophies: culture as objectivation, expression of life (Dilthey), of 'life that rests in the middle' (Spengler), culture at the same time as organic unity of the forming life (Bergson's theory of life) and the observation of these forms of expression as observations of style (Breysig, Lamprecht). The idea *culture = expression*, symbol of a mental realm, is now merely exaggerated and dogmatically posited as universal in a universal symbolics whose fundamental thesis is: Everything that is, is a symbol; a proposition illustrated simultaneously by the principle of functional mathematics: $y = f(x)$.

Spengler neither saw nor solved the problems of contemporary philosophy, that is, those with which it is ultimately engaged, without their being brought out themselves, but merely concealed them anew through a violent generalization, that is, he did not even alter the horizon of the *problems* of philosophy, let alone attaining this horizon itself anew. (Whenever we use the word 'new' in what follows it does not have the meaning of 'never having been' or 'unheard of' and therefore especially worthy of attention and interest, but of 'primordially attained', to be precise, in a specifically philosophical and not cultural or world-historical meaning.) Principally, Spengler amounts to a clever compilation of the major motives of contemporary life philosophies and culture philosophies. It is not only the exaggerated exclusivity of the guild that would like to 'refute' the outsiders by ignoring them, but above all the fact that contemporary philosophy in this clever Spenglerian compilation partially everywhere encounters itself, which makes it understandable that one avoids a fundamental, positive and not just a protectively defensive confrontation and that – leaving aside an easily formulated critique of the somewhat violent skepticism – one does not quite know what to say philosophically. At the same time it also becomes understandable why Simmel could refer to Spengler's book as the most significant philosophy of history since Hegel. It is completely in line with his thinking, which was philosophically, albeit incomparably, more fruitful. A confrontation with Spengler does not come into question for us here; it would, apart from the idea of the universal symbolics, lead back to a critique of life philosophy and of certain motives of culture philosophy. Mentioning Spengler occurred in the interest of pointing to a typical form of the lapsing problem situation. Also this is outside our task.

Mentioning the two major groups of contemporary philosophy is merely supposed to indicate from where an identification of the contemporary problem situation is to be set in motion. We must not be content with this problem situation for its part, as it is in part explicitly or not at all formulated by contemporary philosophy. It is rather to be dissolved into ultimate questions and led back into the origin in order to attain from there a philosophical basic situation and in it the concrete raising of the problems that concern us here.

§ 4 Life as primal phenomenon and the two problem groups of contemporary philosophy

The problem situation is characterized by the deliberately emphasized or merely implicit positing of *'life'* as primal phenomenon. The word must be left in an ambiguity in order to adequately characterize the situation. Biological – genuinely biological or mechanistically corrupted – psychological sense-moments and those specific to the human sciences entwine in manifold accentuation in the meaning of the word. Although, in anticipation of the actual posing of the problems, two major directions in which the meaning is mainly heading are already to be separated:

LIFE AS PRIMAL PHENOMENON

I. *Life* as objectifying, shaping (something), self-expositing [*Aus-sich-heraussetzen*] (and obscurely connected to that something like being, existing *in* this life and *as* such life and increasing it).
II. *Life* as experiencing [*Erleben*], ex-periencing [*Er-fahren*] (it), gathering-in, apprehending, to be precise, the objectified as well as creation itself (and obscurely connected to that, something like being and existing in such life and increasing it).

In these two meaning-directions of 'life' the problem-structure that animates contemporary philosophy must be able to be shown.

(a) Life as objectifying and the problem of absolute validity (the problem of the a priori)

The first meaning conveys the aspect of life as an historical process, as *becoming* and that is as creating and objectifying. The 'epitome of the creations of the spirit' is referred to as culture. For the most part, three 'fundamental creations' are known in accordance with the threefold unfolding of the spirit in a theoretical, practical and aesthetic respect: science, morality and art. In such culture-systems, one by and large does not get clear about religion. Either it is posited as an additional, separate domain of culture or one sees in it merely the reverent forming or incorporation of the three aforementioned domains. Or it is doubted whether it can be regarded as a creation of culture at all; it then, however, remains questionable which independent form of the unfolding of the spirit it should be related back to and how the connection between religion and the domains of culture should be thought. That such difficulties persist and that work is being done in order to overcome them is also a sign of the fact that the domains of culture are not merely considered as historical phenomena – sprouting, growing and decaying formations in their becoming – i.e. not merely historically circumstantially [*historisch-zuständlich*], but with regard to the basic directions of the possible creative self-unfolding of the spirit. Also this could be yet another merely circumstantial consideration of the spirit, a pursuing of its typical forms and directions of forming. Provided however that one speaks of an order, of a reason-complex *of* science, *of* morality, *of* art, *of* religion, more is at stake than a decision about how a factical science, factical morality, factical art, factical religion are factically related to one another in a concrete period of historical becoming, which unitary direction of style of mental expression they follow. It is a direction of questioning that, in terms of its sense, exceeds and *seeks* to exceed historical facticity, namely the supra-historical question about the reciprocal relationships of ultimate ideas and goals for achievement, the question about the system *of* values and about the a priori systematics *of* reason.

Seen from the perspective of this objecthood of what is in itself, of what is valid in itself, which according to its content *consists* of itself and in itself, not on the basis of a relationship to another, by the grace of another, that is, what in such a sense is *absolute, ab-solved*, i.e. free from every relatedness to … and without need of any support and precondition or foundation relationship. Seen from the perspective of this absolute, historical becoming appears as *relative*. The creations of the spirit, which are guided by ideas, of normative values and bound to principles, are in each case a concrete forming, the formed just as much as the forming as a happening and, in the happening having become and being set apart, with concrete means that are available and esteemed at certain times. The relativity and singular uniqueness of every historical culture formation stands opposed to the absoluteness and supra-temporal 'generality' of the idea, of the value and the principle of reason; the factical contingency of the historical stands opposed to the supra-historical necessity of what is valid. *Stands opposed to* – What is meant by this? How is it to be 'thought' that ideas materialize in the objectivations of life, the absolute attains form in the relative and the relative becomes form of an absolute? Is it in the end even an illusion to speak of an absolute? Does not precisely the truly vital aspect of life – life as historical forming, reshaping, shaping anew, demolition, blooming and decay – prove that the assumption of something absolute and something valid is amiss and entirely superfluous? Is absolute validity, 'general validity' not simply an unwarranted naive exaggeration of one's own contingent historical position, 'one's own wrong conclusion projected onto others' (Spengler)?

The development of historical consciousness and therewith the advancement of becoming life as primal phenomenon into contemporary Dasein calls into question the absolute and every purported knowledge of this absolute and its systematics, every so-directed philosophy already prefigured in Plato's doctrine of ideas. We thus have a first problem group that springs from the prevailing of life as primal phenomenon in the first meaning-direction. In the language of contemporary philosophy, this group shall be identified by the problem of absolute validity – of the a priori. Therein are included: questions such as the one about the relation between the relative and the absolute, the problem of history (temporality and supra-temporality), the problem of culture (absolute validity of value and relative forming of goods) and the problem of possible knowledge of the absolute (apprehension of the valid from the relative forms).

For the problem-complex here before us modern Protestant theology offers a good and in many respects direction-giving paradigm. It is the question about the absoluteness of Christianity, about the validity of the claim of absoluteness of the beliefs of the early Christian community, about the absolute meaning of Jesus the person. With the cultivation of the historical consciousness – more exactly the development of history of religions and comparative-religion research – this problem has, for the Christian doctrine and dogmatic, entered a new stage. Earlier, Christianity was, on the basis of a specific metaphysics, simply asserted as the true religion and all the others were declared 'false'. In the Enlightenment the idea of the natural religion of reason was attained that, with regard to every historical individuation, was to contain in itself the proper truth content of religion. From a living historical consciousness, Schleiermacher saw for the first time that the 'absolute element' of religion could not be realized in a single and particular historical religion, but could even less lie in a mere abstract form of reason. The problem that is closely linked to the question about the sense, structure and method of a Christian theology occupied the 19th century and is especially pressing today. With regard to the repeatedly advanced solution that by an extensive in the history of religions comparison the inner value-superiority of Christianity with respect to all other world religions could be secured, it can be objected that thereby the problem is essentially deferred through an incorrect theoretization. Early Christianity did not know any history of religion; it did not attain its faith conviction of the *extra Christum nulla salus* through a history of religions comparison and could not do so because Christianity did not yet have a history.

It was said that the problem was direction giving, since on closer reflection [*Besinnung*] one encounters the questions: first what absoluteness, absolute, means with respect to the relativity of the historically singular [*Einmaligen*], then whether in religion, in art, in the ethical [*Sittlichen*], in science and even in the individual sciences its sense is everywhere the same, further how the sense of 'absolute' is primordially motivated and from where the claim of validity is suggested and with what right 'validity' of this kind is at all assigned to the values and to the principles of reason.

THE PROBLEM SITUATION OF PHILOSOPHY

One speaks of logical, ethical, aesthetic or even religious a priori, of logical and ethical validity as well as of aesthetic general validity and religious absoluteness; in terms of its content it is each time a different a priori, respectively a different validity, but it is nonetheless a priori, validating and a law of reason. The a priori, respectively, the validity is pre-given in the theoretical domain – the validity of truths ($2 \times 2 = 4$) *independently* of the factical enactment of judgment – and this domain is expanded to an a priori lawfulness of reason in general or to an a priori system of values. If one, however, simultaneously with the positing of this a priori objecthood, does not close oneself off to the aspect of history, to vital life, a tension necessarily arises: on the one hand, the a priori, respectively the validity and, on the other hand, the historical relativity of the acknowledgement and denial as well as the contingent singularity of trust and mistrust. Now there is the question about the overcoming of this opposition, respectively, about the resolution of this tension. It is the old Platonic problem, only essentially amplified and complicated through the phenomenon of historical life.

With this also the step towards dialectic appears. One searches for a logic of movement, of becoming, for an historical dynamic in which the oppositions find their justification but at the same time also time and again their overcoming, that is where the concrete singular vitality of history is fully recognized and the supra-temporal idea content of the manifestations is not denied, where the somewhat extrinsic apprehension of ideas as 'measures' of historical knowledge and interpretation is abandoned.

In the mentioned problem group (problem of the a priori, of validity and of history) there hence lies at the same time a motive for the presently ever more strongly advancing tendencies towards a philosophical *dialectic*. It hardly needs to be mentioned that the posing of the problems we have attained up to now is not fully explicated and unambiguous. Indeed, it will simply be necessary to decide whether the conceptual means and the fundamental sense of the conventional posing of the problems of philosophy that pertain here are sufficient or appropriate for such an unravelling of the problems and whether within the framework of transcendental philosophy and dialectic essentially more is to be achieved at all.

LIFE AS PRIMAL PHENOMENON

(b) Life as experiencing and the problem of the irrational (the problem of lived experience)

The pressing-forward of life as primal phenomenon in the second mentioned meaning-direction as the experiencing of Dasein in its intimacy, fullness and obscurity sharply forms another opposition that multifariously intersects and entwines with the previously mentioned direction, namely because in the two meaning-directions of 'life' inheres a basic sense that has so far not been brought out, which – provided that it is *seen* – must radically change the problematic.

For our context, mainly *one* form of the opposition comes into consideration. The surge of the most varied life-forms and life-situations, furthered by the historical consciousness, increased the openness and capacity of feeling for manifold possibilities of Dasein, thereby made immediately available an abundance of attitudinal directions, helped the individual ones to dominantly stand out in relief and led to a pushing-away of previous exclusively dominating ones. The enhanced consciousness of life – constantly enriched anew by history – as conscious experiencing thus caused the merely logical-theoretical attitudinal direction to noticeably recede, which, by virtue of its obvious universality of applicability, always easily sets itself above all others. One attempted to gain clarity about its limits, limits which were going to become apparent above all in a violation of the primordial non-theoretical directions of living experience. This endangering of the predominance of the theoretical simply through the vital and intensified cultivation of qualitatively different possibilities of lived experience could not in the long run leave the structure of the philosophical problematic unaffected. (At the same time it is thereby demonstrated how every philosophy, from the perspective of mere hindsight and afterwards [*Hinterher und Nachher*], becomes fundamentally unfruitful and merely an occupation for academics.)

And even if it ultimately aimed and aims at the a priori, the principles of reason of the creations of the spirit, and sees in this its own and ultimate objecthood, and, according to domains and validity, claims its superiority and adherence to principles over against every other kind of knowledge, then a co-consideration of the creative spirit's directions of forming assigned to those principles and domains of principles, which are differentiated in terms of their aforementioned content, was after all unavoidable. This is all the more the case since all fundamental questions of modern philosophy somehow lead back to the 'I', the subject, consciousness, the spirit, with regard to the manner of ultimate grounding as well as with respect to the predetermination of the systematics. Now, it can be seen more or less clearly today that the research into the forms of lived experience up to this point was either very rough or askew due to the prevailing of the theoretical attitude and unexamined presuppositions; nowhere are such attempts any longer philosophically satisfying. However, provided that philosophy – thus every attempt that is to be set in motion in order to remedy this unsatisfactory situation – should somehow be rational *knowledge*, the question arises for it whether a consideration of living experience that does not immediately and necessarily theoretically disfigure it is possible at all. Philosophy had to raise this objection against itself. Two motives have mainly become effective for this.

First, it is the concept of knowledge in the Kantian transcendental fundamental comprehension. In a formally rough way, knowledge can be defined in this sense as the forming shaping of a (sensation) material, pre-given by the receptivity (passivity) of sensibility, through the spontaneity of the intellect. Everything known is categorially formed material, whereas the forming itself is subject to 'rules' of pure non-empirical consciousness and confers objectivity and validity. The categorially unformed, theoretically unaffected is the merely passively experienced and experience-able [*Erlebte und Erlebbare*]. Nothing can be stated about it, unless in theoretical forming, meaning at the same time, however, the demolition of the immediacy in the mediation through the intellect.

Living experience is first defined as the flow [*Ablauf*] of this logically unaffected, the arising and going-along of the 'I' within this flowing, its releasing-itself, as it were, from the regularity and lawfulness of pure consciousness. Then, contrariwise, precisely the forming itself is grasped according to its sense-content as process and movement, is in all dialectical further developments of transcendentalism often grasped as the proper activity of living experience and life. However, here as well as there the sense of living experience is determined out of the same unitary epistemological-transcendental basic position.

With this concept of knowledge the possibility of a theoretically philosophical apprehension of living experience is argued against, an argumentation that is facilitated by a way of using the term 'living experience', which is, from the outset, ambiguous. The purely sensible receptive 'living experience' is immediate-irrational. Living experience in a wider sense, provided it encompasses all functions and acts in their vital enactment, is the same to a higher degree; this, after all, once again attests to the intensified consciousness of life. A knowledge as forming of this living experience qua living experience means a theoretical shaping, a logical, formally guided mediation of the unmediated immediate, respectively a rationalization of the irrational, a demolition or immobilization [*Stillstellung*] of life in the schema of concepts as the means and results of the forming itself (concept as condensed judgment).

A second motive which Bergson particularly strongly emphasized in his 'An Essay on the Immediate Data of Consciousness' (1889)[1] is taken from language. Knowing communicates itself in language, in words. Language is, it is said, tailored to the spatial external world and its practical, rationally technical control. Both the meanings of words and the concepts relate to space; all logic is logic of space. (These are propositions on which, as alleged discoveries, Spengler today builds up his basic thesis.) Now, provided that also philosophy and philosophical knowing works with concepts and in a communicating way announces itself, all theoretically conceptual apprehension of living experience, of consciousness or of the spirit is a spatialization and therefore a fundamental disfiguration. In addition to the theorizing in general, there is the particular inappropriateness of the conceptual, as something separated in a spatial way with respect to the unspatiality of the mental.

Now, provided that one – analogous to the first opposition between absolute a priori validity and historical relativity – holds on to both elements of the opposition, that is, recognizes the so-called irrationality of life and living experience and at the same time strives for a philosophically (rationally) theoretical knowledge of the spirit in terms of its directions of achievement, one finds oneself confronted with the task of mediating, i.e., of resolving and overcoming the tension between the irrational and rational. With this second problem group, which – again in the language of contemporary philosophy – should be identified as the problem of lived experience, the step towards dialectic reappears: recognition of the oppositions with simultaneously progressing supersession [*Aufhebung*].

This growing tendency towards a dialectical philosophy (historically speaking: the approximation to Hegel), which is mainly motivated in the two problem groups, remains characteristic due to the fact that it posits the elements of the oppositions – that is first 'absolute' and 'relative', respectively the a priori and history and then 'rational' and 'irrational' –

in differing but inessential modifications of meaning like fixed tokens and is now, with the help of dialectic, intent on a dignified unification and supersession of the oppositions. The basic structure of philosophy persists also in the transcendental dialectic, however much it may distance itself from the Hegelian one. Philosophy itself, to which the task of such mediation is properly assigned, can now be taken into consideration as an achievement and phenomenon of life, it can with respect to its possible fundamental positions and opposing elaborations be brought, in a dialectic, to mediated unity, so that it finally suggests itself to expect in dialectical philosophy the universal absolute philosophical knowledge that truly unifies and supersedes within itself the abundance of forms. (Also Spengler's idea of a universal functional symbolics has an unmistakably dialectical tone.) In such a comprehensive dialectic one can also include the legitimate core of phenomenology (culture-philosophical or understanding psychological-circumstantial [*verstehend psychologisch-zuständliche*] observation), provided that a vital seeing and opening-up of unconscious phenomena is assigned to it, an intention towards that, so that the achievement however is in need of actual philosophical treatment. Spengler (*The Decline of the West*) and Jaspers (*Psychology of Worldviews*) have attempted this; the first in a culture-philosophical, the second in an understanding psychological (circumstantial) consideration.

The problem situation is henceforth characterized by the two question groups: (1) the problem of a priori validity, (2) the problem of the irrational. Both are closely and reciprocally connected – irrationality of the historical-contingent, but also the 'irrational a priori' of religion – to the problem of philosophy itself according to idea, basic structure and method.[2] It is not the point to simply take up the problem situation and propose a new solution by means of a new combination and re-modelling or a merely stricter formulation or modification of the sense of some of the fundamental concepts of the schema of the problem. Rather, it should be attempted to loosen the schema itself and as such in order to once again press forward to the idea of philosophy. In doing so it is not that one has become 'tired' of previous philosophy and would now set about thinking up a new system and try out whether it would not be possible, for a change, in this way. It is not decisive whether that which is to be attained is shockingly new or whether it is old, or whether from out of this a system is really to be built or not. Something else is at stake, namely to lead philosophy from out of its alienation back to itself (phenomen-

PHENOMENOLOGICAL DESTRUCTION

ological destruction).[3] (The genuine is always new because the old has always in some sense necessarily become un-genuine for us. I find the genuine only provided that the old is also there, for a certain stretch of the way goes along behind it. It is always somehow in *existentiell* necessity there as enactmental motive in philosophizing.)

§ 5 The phenomenological destruction

At first it is necessary to lead more acutely out of the concrete contemporary situation towards the problem. That can only happen if we first and for a long time speak the language of the problem situation itself. This concerns above all the word 'life' in the two major directions of its fluctuation in meaning. For us the usage is always a formal indication that what is meant by the word should somehow be adopted in the problematic of philosophy.

The leading towards the problem comes about by means of the phenomenological-critical destruction, such that above all the concealed sense-moments come to a philosophical terminus in a manner in which they press towards something decisive. Therein lies, first, if we take destruction into account, now simply with respect to its function in view of historically pre-given philosophy, the recognition and corresponding estimation of the continuity of intellectual history, the 'conviction' (at first) that it is naive to suppose one could today, or ever, start again from scratch in philosophy and be so radical as to dispense with all so-called tradition. In this way it happens that this radicalism (e.g. empiricism, but also rationalism) is merely a retreat into one's own common sense, which always turns out to be a rationalistically diluted and thus 'generalized' contingent spiritual horizon that philosophy will always have to mistrust. The going-back to 'the matters themselves', as it is often expressed in the radicalism of phenomenology, may not be understood in this way. It rather also consists in enacting one's own factical situation ever more primordially and preparing it in the enactment towards genuineness.

(a) The function of phenomenology within the whole of philosophizing

The phenomenological-critical destruction can, however, directly be understood as belonging to the sense of philosophizing so that it loses the appearance of being makeshift and of being the preparation for proper philosophizing. From the outside, its activity at first looks like a critical poking-around at individual concepts and word meanings. One points out ambiguities, contradictions, obscurities, confusions, deficiency in tidiness and astuteness of the conceptual work. Wherever such work is performed in isolation, and this happens not infrequently, it easily gives the impression that phenomenology is word explanation, detection and elimination of equivocations, determination and marking-off of fixed meanings. This conception of phenomenology as a not entirely unproductive cleaning-up in the field of ambiguity and laxity in philosophical and pre-philosophical concepts is fostered by the fact that phenomenology is posited and claimed as the fundamental science of philosophy. In this sense, namely as clarification of the fundamental concepts of logic, it also had its first impact.

One might find this role of phenomenology as fundamental science of philosophy very plausible, especially if one mainly or exclusively moves within it in the sense of a descriptive discipline. It only becomes somewhat indefinite as soon as one poses the question how far this fundamental science ought to extend, how purely and in which structural context the foundations are to be laid and along which 'guideline' the foundation work for philosophy would have to progress in order to be able to begin with the proper philosophy. That is not especially alarming, provided that one has in the background a commonly accepted concept of philosophy, which after all must, as it has always been, be about logic, ethics, aesthetics, and – if one is daring – about philosophy of religion. When more sharply formulating the concept, whether or not consciously explicitly or unknowingly following old philosophical basic directions, divergences then arise, especially if one takes the epistemological basic position as the basis. Thus the sharp and essential opposition between Husserl and the so-called Munich phenomenology is a philosophical one, more exactly, an epistemological one, which, as such, then respectively determines the whole of philosophy. The difficulty however does not consist in whether the 'realistic' or the 'idealistic' transcendental comprehension and orientation asserts itself and can maintain itself against the other, but in whether it is in principle permissible to posit phenomenology as the fundamental science for philosophy without having a radical concept of philosophy. Only from there can its function be determined if one wants to regard phenomenology as such a fundamental scientific pre-discipline at all. Provided that a radicalism of clarification is being strived for in the latter, its own positing is unradical and means a falling-away from the phenomenological basic posture if the concept of phenomenological philosophy and its 'presuppositions' do not grow out of this basic posture itself. It is hopeless to even want to begin to lay solid and appropriate foundations if the construction plan is missing. Or is wanting to lay foundations for a construction not in general an unphenomenological tendency? May the structure of philosophy be 'presented' in this way at all? It would be fundamentally amiss to think that what was said was about the so-called 'critical question', about the necessity of applying it also to phenomenology and of asking: 'How is phenomenology at all possible?', so that the transcendental critique would be seen as prior to phenomenology. This is an argumentation which does not even come close to the primitive sense of the phenomenological basic posture. By the same token, one ought not to conceal from oneself that an initial concrete cultivation of the phenomenological basic posture, a fructification, was necessary in order to have it concretely as a communicated posture, more still in order to attain decisive references for its genuine enactment. Another thing is, however, the immanent explication of its own sense and the characterization directed from there of what it fundamentally is and ought to be. How difficult such a consideration is, Husserl himself shows in the introduction to the first edition of volume II of the *Logical Investigations*, where phenomenology is posited as *descriptive psychology*.

The continuously persisting danger is now that phenomenology is prematurely constricted into pre-given manners and directions of philosophizing; the danger grows with the understandable and necessary tendency to arrive at a philosophy by means of phenomenology (cf. Scheler, who gives the impression that phenomenology is something 'for becoming Catholic'). Therefore what lately breaks through as formal phenomenology is certainly something different from the hitherto known, however, itself not a 'concrete' phenomenology. In this respect, one can rightly and instinctively become suspicious. The question, however, is whether this formal phenomenology does not after all have a sense which is primordially its own and a certain explicative function within the whole of philosophizing, and whether its elaboration in the sense of an a priori science of reason remains merely secondary and phenomenologically not original.[1]

We are led to these deliberations by the attempt to understand the sense of the phenomenological-critical destruction and apprehend it as going beyond a mere word explanation. This questionable business of word explanation does not concern any arbitrary ones but those which express so-called fundamental concepts, e.g. 'representation'; and the meanings are clarified because they are unclear, because different meanings run confusedly through one another, that is because the word itself is 'ambiguous'. In the 'ambiguity', which is always at the same time also afflicted with an indistinctness of the meanings, a multiplicity of meaning-directions is indicated, different meaning-complexes within different logical structure complications are pointed out. The latter themselves carry within them an expressive sense-relation to object areas which, according to their what-character, are more or less genuinely experienced and comprehended.

Already the pursuit of the ambiguity alone is therefore the understanding tracing into diverging directions of meaning. With their differentiation and division a possible characterization of them and of the 'underlying' thing or object domain is given. In the clarification of such words is thus implied, provided that it is genuinely enacted, the unitary over-viewing and co-viewing having-present of the directions of meaning. It means at the same time the having-present of different situations from which the meaning-directions depart and in which they become genuinely pursuable. From this still entirely initial understanding of the sense of the clarification we have to go back to the philosophically primordial basis of enactment from which such clarifying and determining must grow.

(b) The boundedness of phenomenological destruction to preconception

The so-called 'mere word explanation' and plying of 'mere meanings' is a task and an aim that presupposes a rich and only quite specifically accessible situation in which, now, concrete situations must be traversable in which the rudimentary, semi-clear moments of meaning fully distinguish themselves and attain specific contours. It is no blind taking-up of meanings that just happen to fall into one's hands, no merely technical attachment of one of those meanings to a pre-given word form. The danger is certainly there, it is not exactly always and everywhere evaded in phenomenology, and one often catches oneself being tempted to 'tear words out of their context' rather than to expressly take up a meaning from this context, to intuitively fulfil the meaning, and posit that which gives itself there as absolute givenness, without having phenomenologically taken into account the situations and the change of situations for the *sense of relation and of enactment* of such 'meaning-fulfilling acts'. This overlooking is due to the fact that the phenomenon of the situation in itself is phenomenologically still too unfamiliar and is not yet apprehended in its fundamental meaning. Accordingly, also the concrete situations are not to be mistaken for mere 'viewpoints' of the consideration.

As long as this deficiency persists, what is designated as *pre-delineation* also remains blurry. The peculiar thing is in fact that meanings point into contexts; phenomenologically, it is found how in them themselves motives are posited in such a way that these give a direction of the sense-complex. This direction itself brings with it a first loosening-up of the sense-relations and with this loosening-up an intimating and addressing as well as an opening of new direction-laden motives. Therefore, the phenomenon of the 'pre-delineation' must now itself be clarified, that means it must be understood in the phenomenological basic posture, i.e. be traced back to its motives of origin. In this, a decisive task is to show how sense-manifoldness and sense-unity are co-characterized through pre-delineation, more exactly, how the last is 'founded' in the first ones, what foundation means primordially and enactmentally, how unity and manifoldness of sense is understandable as explicated from *existence* [*Existenz*], likewise the 'a priori'. Furthermore it must become understandable how pre-delineations are motivated in the phenomenological basic act of light-disclosing – light: implicit context of sense in an entire pre-aspect – *preconception* which highlights itself by means of philosophical *fundamental* experience (of a world of experience).

Phenomenological destruction – as a fundamental part of phenomenological philosophizing – is therefore not without direction; it does not fortuitously take up meanings of words in order to explain them by means of other taken up meanings. It is not mere shattering but a 'directed' deconstruction [*Abbau*]. It leads into the situation of the pursuit of the pre-delineations, of the enactment of the preconception and thereby of the fundamental experience. From that it is evident that all phenomenological-critical destruction is *bound to preconception* – and therefore not ultimately primordial and ultimately decisive, but presupposes philosophical fundamental experiences.

[Comment:] The meaning of pre-delineation and preconception (how and from where motivated) for philosophical concept formation.[2] 'Pre-delineation', 'preconception', and 'pursuit in the attention-drawing understanding' contrast with the *inductively* (inducing thing-objects) epagogic method. The idea of the epagogic method: from the individual as something 'particular', respectively as an 'instance', to the 'general', to 'genus', respectively to the 'law'. In its characterization one merely considers: starting point and goal, but also these themselves are merely seen in an object-like way according to debit–credit (result). Induction merely means the leading from–to. The sense-genetic process, its genuine theoretical situation, namely the induction of objects and things, then the *theoretical* preconception of object induction and its motives, the borders of the motive-giving situation, elaboration of the last and so forth, all these are not examined, neither the possibilities that exist for such theoretical preconceptions. (Cf. Driesch, On Induction;[3] Nik. Hartmann on experiment in: Philosophical Basic Questions of Biology.[4])

(c) Philosophy and factical life experience

The phenomenological destruction is, by way of contrast, not only a merely secondary and convenient, more easily manageable methodological means for more limited purposes, but is one of the fundamental elements of the phenomenological posture, that is, it belongs to it as such and is to be co-enacted in every phenomenological basic posture, in its 'approach'. Why this is the case shall now be merely intimated.[5] The most proximate reason lies in the fact that philosophy does not consist in deduced general definitions, but is always an element of *factical life experience*. This surely does not mean: Philosophy is not supposed to make constructions and chase after phantasms but should stick to empirical experience, should be 'inductive', should be 'positive'. It means something quite fundamental and does not at all concern the manners and ways of grounding philosophical propositions neither does it concern the restriction of the object domain of philosophy to 'experience' in the sense of empirical experience. What is positively meant becomes accessible only in a thorough consideration of the sense-complex of factical life experience.[6] It should only by way of indication be pointed to here through a characteristic of factical life experience. This is the particular characteristic that I designate as the *fading of meaningfulness*. It is not a disappearing but a fading, i.e. a transition into the stage and into the mode of non-primordiality where the genuineness of the enactment and beforehand the renewal of the enactment are lacking, where even the relations wear themselves out and where merely the content that itself is no longer primordially had 'is of interest'.[7] *Fading* has nothing to do with 'losing something from memory', 'forgetting' or with 'no longer finding any interest in'. The content of factical life experience *falls away* from the

PHENOMENOLOGICAL DESTRUCTION

existence relation towards other contents; that which falls away remains *available*; the availability itself can, however, for its part fade as a sense-character of the relation and pass into that of mere *usability*. ('Fading', 'transition' and so forth are *existentiell concepts*.)

This concerns – as it concerns every content, relation and enactment of factical life experience – also the sciences and philosophy, both according to their 'position' in factical life experience, albeit in different respects and different ways. Scientific and philosophical concepts, propositions and ways of consideration permeate factical life experience more or less comprehensively, however, they do not compose it; in fact they permeate it in the character of the faded, i.e. they have fallen away from the primordial existence relation. Provided that the phenomenological-critical destruction now explicitly directs itself towards factically pre-given philosophies, the latter are subject to the questioning towards the primordiality of the existence relation, further to the question about the extent of the philosophically pure elaboration of the basic concepts and phenomena that are co-given in their approach, their guiding position and their idea and equally to the question about the right pursuit of the pre-delineations which can be brought into relief.

It must, however, be even more sharply distinguished: I. the belongingness of factical life experience *as such* to philosophy and thereby the belongingness of destruction to the 'method'; II. the necessity of taking pre-given philosophy as a starting point is not to be equated with I., only insofar as the respective factical life experience will be somehow permeated, philosophically laden; necessity of the continuity of the problems – of the surely descendant *understanding to be propagated*.

It could now be said: Certainly, philosophy can begin with a critical confrontation and thereby will be referred to the factical situation of intellectual history and in this respect will stand in factical life experience; however, it can dispense with this and immediately construct positively. In contrast, we will see that this is a fundamental illusion and that every philosophy, from its starting point onwards, in some way drags factical life experience along within its problematic – even if in an entirely hidden, un-genuine and heavily theorized way.

For now, it is only a thesis that *factical life experience belongs to the problematic of philosophy in an entirely primordial sense*, namely in a sense that hitherto was concealed and became the reason for many pseudo-problems in philosophy,[8] further in a sense that has nothing to do with the prejudice of positivism and that is a far cry from the thesis that every philosophy has grown from its factical spiritual situation and as such is necessarily and from the outset relative.

(d) The application of the destruction in the two problem groups

The earlier delineated historically factically pre-given problem situation therefore becomes the starting point for the phenomenological-critical destruction. Given the lack of a concrete understanding and the absence of a sufficient explicit interpretation of the *preconceptual* sense-relations to be considered as motivating for the pre-delineations, this destruction can only be intimated, not to mention the fact that it would have to considerably disturb the economy of the lecture course.

When identifying the problem situation we have – apart from the first mentioned opposition between strict scientific philosophy and worldview philosophy which we now provisionally leave in the background – encountered two problem groups, both characterized by the fact that in them 'life' is posited as primal phenomenon. According to the two meaning-directions the word mainly displays, we subdivided: I. the problem of the a priori, respectively of absolute validity, II. the problem of the irrational.

The tension in the problem can be illustrated by means of oppositions; for the first group through the opposition between the relativity and contingency of the historical, on the one hand, and the absolute validity of the a priori of reason and the a priori of value, on the other; for the second group through the opposition between living experience (in the narrow sense) as atheoretical and the knowing of it (as theoretical apprehension of the atheoretical).

It is easy to show that we are not dealing here – provided that there is anything like that at all – with special problems situated on the periphery of philosophy that basically hardly ever touch the core, but that in them philosophy itself is in question as well. In the first group, questions are interwoven like the one about the proper *object* of philosophy, the a priori; then the questions what 'a priori of reason', what 'reason' and 'rational consciousness' would mean, what the structure of the area of the a priori is regarding *content*, how its relation to the singular and relative of history, of empirical factuality in general is to be thought and, finally, in which way – provided that philosophy is supposed to be transcendentally oriented – all these questions are to be built into the problem of consciousness or are to be developed from it; in short: *how it stands with what philosophy is concerned with.*

PHENOMENOLOGICAL DESTRUCTION

In the second group lie questions about the manner of epistemic theoretical seizure of the objecthood in question: whether philosophy, with regard to the totality of life – as forming and experiencing – is not condemned to violence; or whether it does not come especially close to life in as much as it 'demolishes' it; and whether it should and must content itself with ordering life in a system of concepts so that each and everything can be accommodated and thus has its place – a nicely crafted system that does not leave anything outside of itself, that can be judged according to efficacy, economy, acuity of the dialectical composition, beauty, rounded-off-ness and completeness; and finally whether propositions containing subject matter in the sense of the sciences are to be attained which adequately grasp and bring to conceptual expression even the object of philosophy; in short: *how it stands with the manner and method in which philosophy works on its object.*

A further question would be the one as to whether both groups can be treated separately and why not. Both question groups spring from one root, the primal phenomenon of life; whether genuine or not remains an open question.[9]

The mentioned oppositions are obviously meant to designate specific phenomena, even though the degree of formulation in terms of meaning is different. We leave these phenomena themselves on the very bottom of the primal phenomenon and follow some main lines of their sense-according pre-delineations in order to thereby attain the centre of the questioning. It still remains to be seen, however, how far, and if at all, it will be addressed as the centre of the entire philosophical problematic.

We will take from each problem group *one* phenomenon as well as the co-given ambiguities 'circulating' around it, which is sufficient for the present purposes, although it is hardly sufficient for the task of philosophy: 1. initial specification of the ambiguity, 2. first bringing-out, 3. pursuit of the pre-delineations, 4. understanding of the preconception.

PART ONE

On the destruction of the problem of the a priori

§ 6 The six meanings of history and first bringing-out of the pre-delineations in them

The most blatant phenomenon, as it were, in the first problem group that endangers the a priori, or absolute validity, the object of philosophy, is *history*.

By the word 'history', we mean different things – meanings that all, however, point back to a unitary sense-complex:

I. When I say: 'My friend studies history' or, as the beautiful expression has it, 'He majors in history', then I mean history and not law or natural sciences; here, history means *science of history*.
II. Someone is working on a philosophical problem, he is given the advice: 'Just orient yourself a bit in the history!', i.e. on the factual realizations of the work on the problem. Or one says: 'He is not very versed in actual philosophy but he is an excellent authority on the history.'
III. One speaks of 'history-less' tribes and peoples and means they have no history. It does not mean they have no science of history or that their ancestors did not really exist; equally, it also does not mean that they are not the product of previous factuality; rather one means they have no *tradition*.
IV. Again, in a different way one speaks of 'history' as life's great instructor, e.g. for *politics*.
V. One means something else when one says 'This city has a very turbulent history.' Or 'This person has a sad history.'

VI. I may ask e.g.: 'What kind of story [*Geschichte*] is that again?' Or one says: 'A very unpleasant story [*Geschichte*] happened to me.'

By merely stating the ambiguities nothing is achieved; what matters is to exercise the so-called pre-understanding, to understand the sense as it is factically meant, i.e. to put oneself into the *situation* in which such statements are factically enacted in order to thus gain the possible perspective in which the moments of sense that predominate and lead further can be brought out.

We now attempt a first bringing-out of the pre-delineations located in the ambiguities, in fact, still in the comprehension and explication that stays within the ambit of the understanding in factical life experience:[1]

I. 'He studies history' in the sense of the science of history. With history something *definite* is factically meant – in factical life experience co-given with it in its life-context – however, in the character of indefiniteness. What is meant by this indefiniteness? I know of someone that he studies history in the first semester. I can explicate this opinion by bringing to mind that he always goes to the seminars of Finke and Below, sits in the library and carries large codices home with him, works on medieval papal documents; one never sees him working in the natural sciences institutes. That is a rough explication in the style of factical life experience. One can pursue it further. Studying history is after all not simply reading, collecting, excerpting, acquiring knowledge; it is a wanting to grow into a method, into a goal-directed acquisition of knowledge that occurs in going through certain provisions of the individual steps of knowledge. The study of the science of history is accompanied by the study of the historical past. Studying history therefore means to make the historical world accessible to oneself, but in the form of growing into historical research as science. The stress is on the latter when I say that he studies history and not theology and also not natural science. In I., history functions therefore in the sense of a science (concrete logic and so forth, accessible in a theoretical attitude).

II. If it is said of someone that 'He is not very versed in philosophy itself but he is an excellent authority on the history, he is very cognizant of the history', then the present meaning of the word points towards *what* is historically established in such and such a way, *what* in the past was such and such, *what* 'happened' there, *what* was taught there, *what* kind of views *'were'* held about the different problems: a *field of facts* is directly meant without aiming at the manner of its representation, its knowledge.

III. The talk about 'history-less tribes and peoples', be it justified or not, again means something different by the word 'history': tribes *without history* do not publish editions of public documents, do not write down an account of their past.[2] This does not mean that those tribes are lacking a developed science of history, the factical possibility of also having available in their factical life experience the access to a certain theoretical attitude towards a certain domain of subject matter. They are without history – neither means that with respect to their Dasein, the Dasein of the tribe, there was no earlier time, that in general nothing happened to them in earlier times, that nothing happens with them, that nothing occurs in which it was in such and such a way, maybe just as today. Those who are living now are the later ones of earlier ones, they have an earlier time in which they were in such and such a way, but they have no history. It means that they have no *tradition*, they do not 'feel' *as* the later ones of earlier ones. The past for them is not a character in which they factically live and which somehow permeates the content of their life experience; they do not cultivate the past. The history-less tribes do not live in situations that are pervaded by estimations and the inclusion of the meaningful past into the factical circle of life – even if only latently and by habit. They live each day as it comes, according to what the day may bring. They also have no future, no tasks. Conversely, what they did and lived likewise does not interest them. And they are also indifferent to the achievements as present which to them is a detached result that is 'over'. (Later we shall see to what extent one can then speak of a-historical 'being' and further of 'anti-historical' being, whether in both cases 'historical' refers to the same sense-complex.) – The interpretation that they do not *know* their own past also misses the meaning. For one can 'have' a very rich tradition, i.e. one can live out of it and from it without actually knowing the past as a subject matter. Mostly this is precisely not the case.

IV. *Historia vitae magistra*. Use of the word 'history', the instructor of life, means neither history as the science of history nor history as domain of subject matter or as known domain of subject matter – fact, i.e. the objective content as correlate of scientifically historical knowledge. But neither does it mean history in the sense of 'tradition'. Those meanings may all or can all, more or less distinctively, be adopted also in the meaning of the use of the word in question, however, they do not constitute this meaning itself and do not hit on *its* own, that which is *proper* to it. What is meant is the past, namely seen from a quite specific tendency alive in factical life experience, the past in the character of a particular relatedness to this tendency. This particular relatedness has the character of availability belonging to factical life. History – not one's own tradition, but precisely the other, alien tradition – is supposed to give instructions for present-day life, provided that the latter is itself striving for something. For the active politician, history – not only political history in the narrow sense, but the past to a broader extent in terms of content – may absolutely but does not necessarily have to be vividly available, and precisely not in the manner of a merely theoretical taking-note and subsequent drawing of conclusions towards a use of what occurred in the sense of a warning or positive guidance. Rather, it may be available in such a way that in and from his factical political life the past is fully familiar to him and that he operates also from out of this past, so that this very familiarity with history itself determines every new historical experience.

V. In sentences like 'This person has a sad history' or 'This city has a very turbulent history', the word 'history' again has a particular meaning, one that is in a certain way connected to the ones previously discussed. One is tempted to say here that history is synonymous with 'past'. What 'past' means is at first comprehensible, namely in the rough and diffuse manner of factical use. But does the first sentence only mean that this person has a past and this past is now precisely a sad one, that is, that he differs from other people in this respect, as far as the human being is simply something which 'becomes', in a development, in a temporal process that can be characterized in this way or another? Or does 'having a past', 'having a history', mean something new with regard to the previously mentioned meanings of history, so that by inserting the previously mentioned meanings into the word combination one does not hit on what it primordially and genuinely means? Apparently; that already roughly becomes clear when we try to go through the previous meanings, even if they are not at all precisely determined yet. 'Having a history' does not mean 'having a science of history'. Neither does it mean 'having' the historical past as domain of subject matter. It does not mean having

SIX MEANINGS OF HISTORY

tradition. Furthermore, it does not mean: having a history as being familiar, in the characterized manners, with the historical past. Or being familiar with one's own history, the history that the respective person 'has'. (For the time being, it is only important that you become attentive and come into the situation where you hit on something, i.e. where something unique announces itself.)

VI. And, finally, the use of the word in a seemingly trivial meaning. I say: 'That's a fine mess' [*Das ist mir eine schöne Geschichte*] or 'A very unpleasant story [*Geschichte*] happened to me today'. In this case history means 'incident', 'occurrence', in fact an incident in which I myself am somehow involved, which concerns me.

It is therefore necessary to put oneself into the indicated situations of understanding the temporally particular meaning and to do so without attempting to explain and without prejudices in terms of a logic of history or epistemological prejudices; we must understand the meanings in their concrete indefiniteness which is after all each time a particularly characterized one.

What should happen now after this initial specification of the ambiguities, after the first bringing-out of the meaning-complexes that are particular each time? There are different individual meanings or individual cases. One may be tempted to search for the common – that is, for what history means in general – in order to then order and subdivide the cases as special differentiations. One sees immediately that it does not work like this. One is automatically led to ask from where those different meanings each time attain their sense and where the primordial sense lies of all these indicated meaning-complexes, that is, the 'origin' from which they grow. The question is not asked as to how it factically came about, which were the factically present reasons that account for the fact that the meanings diverge like this, but rather the question wherein the originary motives for the genesis of those sense-complexes lie.

We now once again take up what has been provisionally brought out and more sharply pursue pre-delineations that can be encountered, which amounts to an explication of the sense-complexes. How far we will go in this is determined by the circle of the guiding tasks.

DESTRUCTION OF THE PROBLEM OF THE A PRIORI

§ 7 The right pursuit of the pre-delineations: the explication of the sense-complexes

ad I

History in the sense of science of history: That means a complex of tasks for theoretical knowing from which tasks this knowing is determined into particular methods. These tasks and these methods are in a certain way accessible in factical life experience. The access stipulates special attitudes that may be different from that of factical life. What is meant by history there can and must primordially be understood as a complex of manners of comportment of experiencing and achieving. If one asks *whereby* it is exactly that which can be designated as science of *history* and not another one, from where the determination originates, then it turns out that for this it is *co*-determining what science is concerned with, what it is about – history; just as natural science is science of nature. At least one usually likes to make both sciences understandable by using this comparison. Whether justifiably or not we do not have to investigate here. (History as concrete logic.)

ad II

History, it is said, means something *objective*: that which has occurred, the past, that which is past. By this is meant in the broadest compass everything that has ever occurred. We will not go into the question as to whether all that occurred is already historical or whether the historical only constitutes an extract from what occurred. In any case, it is about facts, events, people, cultures and so forth that factically once existed. It is about something which can be characterized according to its what-content, something which according to its what – according to what is known about it – stands in no connection with what history means in the I. sense, namely a complex of theoretical, methodologically guided manners of comportment. For example, an *event* in the life of Jesus (the raising of Lazarus) has according to its what-content not the faintest relationship to the historical source criticism in New Testament exegesis, that is, for example, with the division between a synoptical and johanian tradition. I do not need to be an historian, i.e. I do not need to have available the attitudinal complex and procedure-complex defined by the science of history and can still know history, perhaps much more intimately, vitally, and more comprehensively than a professional historian. However, history as that which is past still requires, in order to be known, a certain manner of experiencing, of apprehending, apart from every scientific activity.

History as a specific theoretical attitudinal complex points back to what it is oriented to, i.e. to a domain of subject matter.

History as the past, as an objectively precedented totality ('meant in the idea') requires a certain manner of experiential access. In this, the *domain of subject matter* of history as science of history does not need to coincide with history as the universal past, neither regarding content nor with regard to the manner and scope of the theoretical elaboration. If we ask what centrally determines this totality of being in terms of content, where the fullness of that which is past leads back to, then the answer is: *Human beings*, individuals and communities, standing in certain systems of effects, are bearers of what is generated. One can bring the latter as objectivations, manifestations or symbols of human reality into a fundamental relationship with this human reality as the centre, a relationship of being which in actual occurring and being-past itself also occurs and has also passed.

The further meanings of the word 'history' apparently present themselves as certain determinations, deductions and mixings of the two previously mentioned meanings: history in the subjective and history in the objective sense.

ad III

It is often the custom to also designate history-less peoples and tribes as 'barbaric'. In this context, history was already more closely defined as 'tradition'. It should be noticed in which context this meaning stands. One says: A people, a community of people 'has' no history. According to that, history is something that is 'had' or not 'had'. Provided that history-less is equated with barbaric, the 'having' and 'not having' is subject to an evaluation: the having of history is considered to be an advantage. This 'having' or 'not having' must presumably be a special relationship that requires clarification. Schematically, one can attempt to firmly insert the previously mentioned meanings into the meaning-complex in question. A people 'has' no history in the sense of science of history. The Middle Ages, for example, had no science of history, however, in its life it obviously had a rich tradition, e.g. precisely in its central direction of life, in the religious. It therefore had history and accordingly history here does

DESTRUCTION OF THE PROBLEM OF THE A PRIORI

not mean science of history. Likewise having does not mean here being in possession of something, in this case: having an attitudinal complex available. ('Having' a science means: 'possessing', possessing possibilities of access as factical ones co-given in factical existence; factical *being-available* and factical entering into a certain attitude.)

[Let us choose another insertion:] A people has no history in the sense of a 'past'. However, a tribe of Zulu natives does have a past and yet 'has' no history. The difficulty lies in the meaning of having. When I say the tribe has history and yet has none, the first 'having' means *the relationship* of the objectively thingly having-coming-to-it [*objektiv gegenständlichen Zukommens*] or not having-coming-to-it. The tribe is something that really is, which as something real is subject to becoming: which today has so-and-so many tribe members, which decades ago had another chief etc.; something that inherently changes. We can therefore say: A people has no history (science of history) and still has history. Or we can say: A people has history (as past) and still has no history.

The having in 'having history' or 'not having' is a (formal) relationship in which the one element of the relationship, the tribe, does not function or is meant as an object, but as a *subject* that in a particular and differing way can 'have' or 'not have' something. What does 'having' and 'not having' now mean in our case? Is it distinctly characterized or merely just as roughly indirectly described when it is said: being in possession of something past; as a subject having this and that available; having the possibility of making the past accessible to oneself at any time, of taking note of it? Provided that a tribe knows about yesterday's successful hunt, something past is available to it, in its possession. The Dasein of the tribe is such that past things are available to it and it makes use of the availability. That is the case when the tribe draws lessons from the latest hunt. Nevertheless, the tribe does not 'have' *its* past. The relationship of this 'having' is still in need of a qualitative determination. The having expresses: a *preserving*, in one's own becoming Dasein itself, of what has become *as* something which has become *of this one's own becoming* (in becoming co-having and constantly having anew). Preserving of one's own Dasein *in its achievements*: culture (not so much *the* having been existent therein); in preserving there *is* the rhythm of one's own Dasein or this rhythm *is* at the same time such a preserving as well, it belongs to it. The characterized relationship therefore also belongs to the innermost Dasein itself and is no mere possible attitudinal complex, something that is not externally attached to Dasein. From this particular Dasein-immanent relationship of having – as preserving and cultivating one's *own* past and precisely *being there* [*dasein*] with this preserving itself – the word 'history' receives its specific meaning. It is no determination or derivation of I. (perhaps exactly the other way round), but neither is it a merely quantitatively limiting one of II., as if it were merely about the past of the tribe as a small excerpt of the totality of being of what has occurred and not about *the* past that can objectively be assigned to a people – the occurring that *it* has merely gone through and has, as it were, left behind, no other one – but about its *own* past which it 'has' as its own in the mentioned proper 'relation' and *'is'* in *this* having.

We now know:

Having in the sense of having-coming-to-it, *objectively*; object relationship, correlate of theoretical determining.
Having as the having available (factically) of attitudes; possessing the aptness [*Eignung*] to make accessible to oneself.
Having related to the past as one's *own*; 'preserving' more than remembering, recalling, thinking of it; one's *own* past *plays into* one's own Dasein (this, however, in a specific manner).

ad IV

At first, one might assume that in the meaningful whole *historia vitae magistra*, the first meaning, that is, history as science of history, had its proper place, namely in the sense that it has an enlightening effect, gets errors and prejudices out of the way and that it does so precisely through the rigour of its critical work, i.e. through critical inspection and evaluation of the sources as well as through critical interpretation, that is, through moments that characterize this theoretical attitudinal complex as such. That is, however, not the primary meaning. The primary meaning aims at the fact that the past – that which already occurred as such according to its *what-content* as something that in fact occurred – is supposed to give instruction for future conduct. Also here the past as totality of being is therefore put into a relationship to future conduct. The latter is such in a factical life experience with its more or less sharply highlighted tendencies. From these the past comes alive and from there it receives a distinction, related to Dasein, provided that it for its part sets itself in a distinctly directed way to the outside [*nach außen setzt*] and seeks to achieve something.

DESTRUCTION OF THE PROBLEM OF THE A PRIORI

Provided therefore that here history as objective past comes into a relationship to factical life experience and in a certain manner plays into the latter, it is appropriate to confront this relationship with the previously mentioned one and to ask whether it is not fundamentally the same. However, *one* difference can be grasped straight away: In III., we are dealing with an immanent relationship of Dasein to *one's own* past which was lived by oneself. It is not an arbitrary what-content of what is past but a specific one, determined by the actual Dasein, from the latter the playing-into is motivated and also determined. This is not the case where the past is the instructor for a politician. It is certainly the past in a specific accentuation, namely, past political life, however it is not the past of the politician himself. What is therefore meant here by past has *a looser relationship* to actual Dasein, however much exactly the what-content of the past, with respect to the character in which it is 'had', is motivated from the what- and *goal-content* of the factical tendencies of actual Dasein *and varies with those tendencies and interests*. It is a looser relationship that does not necessarily touch on Dasein as such and perhaps cannot touch upon it at all. It is, however, a nonetheless latent relationship in this Dasein, latent of course not in the immanence of the previously mentioned relationship. It is not that the factically living active political human being at a remove here and there consults history, just makes some inquiries, takes note of this and that. But neither is it that the taking note, as it were, goes on incessantly, as if he were actually continuously occupied with the past, which would really make political activity impossible in his own present. It is the relationship of being-familiar with a past that is not one's own, which is distinguished by actual tendencies of Dasein, a past interpreted on the basis of these tendencies and simultaneously giving them guidance, which in 'instructing' them recoils back on them. Having is related to a past that is not one's own, which is however a being-familiar-with accentuated by one's own actual tendencies of Dasein and *guiding these*, the being-familiar of which distinctly motivates the actual tendencies.

ad V

In the sentence 'This person has a sad history', the relationships which we already discussed in III. are discernable once again. There it became necessary to distinguish between 'having' in the sense of 'having-coming-to-it', 'belonging to' [*zukommen, zugehören*], respectively 'not having-

RIGHT PURSUIT OF THE PRE-DELINEATIONS

coming-to-it', 'not belonging to' and 'having' as 'possessing', 'having at one's disposal' and 'having' as newly taking along and preserving one's own past in one's own Dasein. The first meaning of 'having' that designates an object-thingly [*objektgegenständliche*] relationship first seems to be located in the sentence in question: a sad past inheres in this person. We immediately notice that this paraphrase does not fully express the intended meaning of the sentence. We want to say *more* than in sentences such as: the lectern has a brown colour – the cathedral steeple has scaffolding on it; also more than what is to be found in sentences such as: the waiter has an old cap – the girl has blond braids; these sentences already mean 'more' than the first mentioned ones. We want to say something different than in sentences such as: the mother has a headache – my brother has the conviction that a mistake was being made here – the young man has a high opinion of himself – this man has good taste – that man has a liking for children – this person has a sad history. It should be borne in mind that we factically talk like this and factically understand what is meant in spite of the monotony of the wording 'have'. One would like to simply schematically order the different meanings in such a way as to say that in the first cases it was about an unconscious having-coming-to-it, in all the other ones about a *conscious* having and this *conscious* having would be *also meant* in the sentences. With the last remark we touch on something correct although the 'conscious' having does not mean anything at all since the differences remain. This 'conscious having' must be clarified and understood precisely according to its primordial meanings, while it must be strongly doubted that the use of the word 'conscious' accomplishes anything at all and does not rather confuse or unilaterally determine the consideration.

We now attempt it in part only in a single case: 'He has a sad history'. In this case, 'having' means more than 'having-coming-to-it' so what is meant is: it belongs to him *to* **have** a past, whereas 'having' has now another meaning than 'having-coming-to-it'. And only if we clarify this specific 'having' will we be able to understand what the word 'history' means in this context. In relation to this, it is appropriate to take up the thread from III. As it did there, having apparently expresses a relationship that is rooted in the Dasein of the having person itself, that therefore is not merely attached to it and touches on it from the outside. Is it sufficient to say that the relationship is a being-familiar of the one who is there [*des Daseienden*] with his own past, that it is latently there and effective, only that here it is one's own past and not, as in IV., one that is

DESTRUCTION OF THE PROBLEM OF THE A PRIORI

essentially not one's own, alien? That the past is one's *own* must be held on to as a characteristic moment, whereby, however, nothing is said yet about the relationship. The relationship of the 'having one's own past' is not yet that of the being-familiar with it in such a way that with this having a functioning of the past that gives instruction and guidance would be motivated. This relationship can certainly also exist, however then, as it were, only on the basis, in the medium of *the* relationship that we are looking for right now.

It was said earlier that the relationship IV. was a 'looser' one with regard to the one noted in III. The latter was characterized as a preserving that takes along and in becoming a preserving-anew of what passes by and has passed by in becoming, namely that of one's own past so that one, as it were, lives in one's own tradition which Dasein gives to itself. One quickly sees that even also this relationship, although it is one that is more intimate to Dasein, is not sufficient for the characterization of what we have in mind as 'having one's own past'. And on closer inspection it also turns out that indeed the relation in III. is not one that is purely (immanently) related to the self-world but is a circuitous one; it runs across one's own achievements, creations and consolidations *in* which one and *with* which and *for* which one partly lives. It is a preserving of the formed environing world, the determinate with-world and the forms of with-world living and with-world having, even also and precisely a preserving of the objectified life accomplishments in their relationship to the self-world. On the way *across these* forms, experienced and formed in becoming Dasein, as those of the life-world, one's own past is preserved. This circuitous relationship is not detectible in the 'having one's own past'. It is a relationship that is different from all previous ones and, unlike any of those already discussed, presses directly towards the self-world. Therefore we are not dealing with it insofar as it lives in its Dasein while achieving in the meaningfulness of the environing and with-world, but rather insofar as it is about it itself.

That also announces itself in the sentence that served as our point of departure: This person has a very sad history. No matter with which purpose the sentence may be spoken: in order to characterize the person in question, to arouse sympathy for him, to solicit help and mercy for him, the 'sad' indicates and refers to the history, insofar as it is the ownmost of the person, insofar as it thereby concerns and touches him himself in the innermost. 'Sad' can mean he was thrown back and forth a lot, he found himself torn inside, he did not mature and did not find himself. It concerns the becoming of the self-world and its tendencies towards and to itself. The 'having one's own past' is based in the innermost self-worldly directed tendencies and aims at the past as what was earlier, as the yet still vital part of one's own self-proper [*selbsteigentlichen*] tendencies at the time. In this way this relationship of having is indeed brought into relief against all others, but it is in itself not yet fully characterized.

ad VI

In the last locution the word 'history' does not express so much that the occurred has occurred, i.e. is something that is past, but that something 'happened', i.e. something occurred that somehow concerns *me*. History here rather pertains to a distinguished occurring, distinguished through the more or less highlighted relationship to me myself or generally to a concrete self-world or further still to a factical environing world complex. History as a distinguished occurring that goes beyond the mere incidence as well as the process-like, beyond a mere flowing. History is then something that does not sink down to mere occurring but is an occurring in the character of meaningfulness, i.e. an occurring that *happens*, 'passes by' the self-world and with-world *in their* environing world.

Let us now summarize the six more sharply brought-out meanings in their references in order to then articulate them even further – at first in *one* direction – as sense-complexes:

I. History as theoretical attitudinal complex, as concretizing logic of a domain of subject matter.
II. History as that which is past, that which has occurred in its totality; a whole of being as something that has become, within the latter the historical in the narrow sense, i.e. especially according to the what: the human being as individual and standing in a community in systems of achieving with its objectified achievements in becoming and having become.
III. History as one's own past in the correlate of the preserving and constantly self-renewing taking-along: tradition.
IV. History as past which is not one's own, which is, however, accentuated through actual, non-specifically self-worldly directed tendencies of Dasein in the correlate of the being-familiar that takes guidance from itself.[1]

V. History as ownmost past in the correlate of a 'having' that is motivated in only self-worldly directed tendencies.
VI. History as occurring in the event character [*Ereignischarakter*] of factical life related to factical self-world, with-world and environing world.

§ 8 Characterization of relation: the articulation of the sense-complexes according to the sense of relation

Although the different meanings have now become unmistakably distinguishable from one another and no longer present themselves as pre-meanings but as sense-complexes that are unarticulated, preferably, however, roughly comprehended in a direction of sense – content, relation and enactment – phenomenologically everything still remains in a rough state. We now attempt a first and specific, initially one-sided articulation, in as much as we pursue the genuine forms and manners of the being-experienced, i.e. the manners of access to what and how it is meant in the mentioned meanings. This relationship of access we call *relation* [*Bezug*]. The relationship is something sense-according, something that contains sense; we therefore speak of the *sense of relation*. The consideration itself shows immediately that the isolation of the sense of relation, that is, of a sense direction within the actual whole of a sense-complex, is only such provided that it is seen according to the facticity and carrying-out of the initiation [*Anhub*] and the continuation of the consideration itself which, considered objectively temporal, presents itself as a set-apart, isolating and piecemeal one.

Instead of abstract and washed-out discussions about the sense-complex and the sense directions within it (sense of content, of relation, and of enactment), we pursue the concrete relations of the pre-given sense-complexes.

The question about the genuine relations, that is, about the manners in which each time that which is meant by history in the various cited cases can be genuinely experienced as such, seems to be already decided. Especially if we consider cases III., IV. and V. it turns out that we have virtually characterized what is meant by history there *by the manner in which it is* **had**, is experienced. That which is referred to as history was in each case determined as a correlate of this and that relation characterized in that way. We have already worked with the sense of relation when we were characterizing; we were involuntarily pressed to do so, which points

CHARACTERIZATION OF RELATION

to a belonging-together in terms of subject matter. Only the I., II. and VI. meanings still remain! In the last one, it was at least intimated that what is meant by history is no mere occurring, but in and as occurring we understood that in which interest is taken; an occurring equally as correlate of a certain taking-interest.

In case I. our question appears to be altogether superfluous. What is meant by history there we defined as an attitudinal complex – that itself is a relation according to its what – so that 'history' here is the expression of a sense of relation, of one, in fact, which already has a rich structural elaboration, which we indicated by the discussion about the *theoretical* attitudinal *complex*. Apparently, however, also to this intended what – the relation – itself there is a manner of access, of having. It can itself, roughly speaking, be a correlate of a relation and in this respect it is easily made plausible that also with regard to a relation the question about the relation to it can be posed.

Formally (based on argument) all this is easily understandable. Relation is something and as such it stands for its part in a possible relation that is already indicated by the fact that I speak of, 'reflect on' and judge it. Precisely here, however, it becomes apparent how the formal instruction easily goes wide of what is in question in terms of subject matter. What is in question is the genuine relation, but also this can still be misunderstood (genuineness and existence). By this one can understand the manner of the attitude that I must adopt in order to objectivize a relation as relation for myself in such a way that I can make statements about it as it itself is. In this way, one takes the view that every relation qua relation belongs to a special class of objects – that of relations – which themselves as such require a general manner of access that then would be the particular relation genuinely belonging to relations in general. That is perhaps one possible way of considering it. However, it must be contested that we are speaking here of the genuine relation to the relation.

That this is not the case here, we now have to show. In doing so, we at the same time illustrate with one concrete case how a constant danger of lapsing into false directions of consideration is tied to the universal meaning and indispensability of the formal indication, furthermore the meaning of genuineness defines itself more closely. (Formal indication, its usefulness and its danger: a sign that maybe the determination of the formal is not quite cleared up yet. The *pre-formal* something! *Genuineness*.)

What is in question is the genuine relation to the concrete relation:

history as theoretical attitudinal complex. We have paraphrased 'relation' with 'manner of being experienced', 'manner of access'; we also said: 'of being had'. This way of speaking is already beguiling, all the more so when I say the relation whose relation to it is in question is something, is an object. By means of this, the question about the relation to the relation is from the outset bent into the one about the manner of the apprehension-like access to the relation as thing [*Gegenstand*], as object [*Objekt*] of epistemic theoretical apprehension, such that this question about the sense of the manner of theoretical objectification [*Vergegenständlichung*], of experiencing as theoretical apprehending, is taken for the only possible question about the relation to the relation.

And even if one understood so far – which already happens rarely – that the apprehension of the relation is a different one than any other thing- and object-apprehension [*Gegenstands- und Objekterfassung*], one would not yet have arrived at the genuine sense of our question. The question about the genuine relation does not coincide with the one about the genuine theoretical relation of apprehension to the relation. But what else then could be meant? If we clarify the discourse about the relation to the relation by means of the discourse about the manner of the being-had of the relation, then a problem domain opens up. We say preliminarily roughly: The relation is had *in* the enactment. Now one asks: *Who* has? What does this having in enacting mean? What does enactment mean? (The [genuine] having of the 'relation' in enactment is no general manner of apprehending, as if the 'enacting' were an indifferent index of all factically had relations.)

With this referring of the relation to the enactment only one problem is indicated against which, from the outset, there either exists a number of objections or which in general one would rather not accept as a serious philosophical problem, in as much as one says: it is simply self-evident that each relation as an actual one simply has to be enacted and that every attitude must be realized if it is to be a real one and that each intentional relationship is one of an act and every act is an act of the 'I' that 'enacts' it. This is not only trivial but even irrelevant for the actual philosophical consideration, in as much as for it the actual factical enactment of the 'empirical', 'factical', 'psychological' or 'anthropological' subject, i.e. the enactment in its factical concretion on the side of the concretion in its now, here and such, is disengaged. In the sphere of theoretical acts and enactments of acts it is not about a concrete enactment of judgment but about the judging consciousness in general,

CHARACTERIZATION OF RELATION

the pure *form* of judging. One does not see that here, with the formal consideration, the enactment is already disengaged; everything else is psychologism and leads out of philosophy into empirical establishing of facts. By resisting the anthropological, also all the problems of existence were once again forced out of philosophy, although they are something essentially different.

For now, it remains an assertion if we attribute to the enactment a special meaning that, in fact, perhaps goes beyond the factual and trivial state of affairs that all acts simply are enacted and that philosophically 'appraises' the enactment and what is connected with it differently than is normally the case.

In our particular case – the question about the relation to the theoretical attitudinal complex (history) as relation – we now merely say: this *relation* is the enactment of this attitudinal complex. Although it should be said that here we only provisionally use attitude and relation as having the same meaning [*äquivok*]. Every attitude is a relation but not every relation is an attitude. 'Attitude' undergoes a genuine determination.

We said that in III., IV., V. and, finally, in VI., that a characterization directed at the relation, the manner of having, was already given with the rough clarification and bringing-out of the sense-complexes. In case I., it is merely indicated as a particular problem. Now case II. still remains. Here relation was not at all an issue at first, in as much as the meaning of the word means precisely: history as objective past, that which occurred as such, in as much as according to its having-been facticity and what-content it is free from the relationship to attitudinal complexes (e.g. an event in the New Testament and its exegesis).

However, one will now easily point out that this objective totality of being is nothing if it is not the correlate of an apprehending, even if not of an actual one, then at least of a possible one. This way the discourse is easily misunderstood. It could be thought that the objective being-past was and consisted in the possible becoming apprehended as past, so that objectively only that would have occurred which as such and in as much as it would as such have become and could become accessible to a corresponding apprehension. It requires a particular kind of relation not as something past but as an object of historical understanding.

In this way, history, in the sense of objective past, would therefore be without relation and would only offer the possibilities of access, to be precise, of the theoretically scientifically historical access, or of the educational taking note, of narrating and recounting. History would,

DESTRUCTION OF THE PROBLEM OF THE A PRIORI

therefore, be something that keeps itself open for possible relations of apprehending, that it, however, does not require; that moreover, according to its content, is not related to a specific present and does not bear within itself the difference between one's own and an alien past. History as this objective totality of being is not necessarily related to a specific actual Dasein.

The objective past: what has occurred thought as detached from any specific relation of historical apprehension, out of a specific historical present. 'Thought as': what is meant is therefore something thought, correlate of a being-thought, not according to its being real but according to its being a thing [*Gegenstand*] and being an object [*Objekt*]. The thinking in this manner is a theoretical determination, more exactly the positing of an *idea*, here that of history as past being. Most of the time it is the case that the content of the idea still extends itself from past occurring via every present and future occurring because as occurring it indeed passes by and becomes something that has occurred, that is, becomes history and exists in the extension of the idea as history.

As little as there can be found a specific concrete relation of a specific concrete Dasein to what is meant here by history – so that it can be said that it lies in the intended sense precisely to keep oneself free and open for possible relations – just as clearly it turns out that what is meant is, with regard to its elaboration of being an object, a correlate of a theoretically idealizing determination that disregards every specific present. Accordingly, this must also be valid for the genuine relation to this occurring. It is likewise an *ideally conceived relation* of an ideal subject, which, as it were, stands completely outside this objective's occurring, of what is past and of what is to come, for which in the end past and future also fade. What is meant by history is detached from any concrete existing [*daseienden*] present – a purely speculative idea. (It excludes a definite, genuine relation to concrete Dasein so that one can only speak of an objectifying [*vergegenständlichenden*] relation of apprehension.)

By contrast, the genuine relation in III., IV., and V. has the peculiar character that only in it and through it that which is meant by history receives its concrete sense, i.e. that the relation for its part points back to a concrete Dasein and that, in the latter, by virtue of the relation, what is meant by history factically exists. The three cases are again different insofar as the relation is, with varying strength, tied to Dasein in which it is alive, in which it is varyingly 'primordial' and thus what is meant by history has a more or less loose relationship to this Dasein itself.

The relation is therefore, according to the level of immanence from which it, according to its sense, necessarily starts out in a concrete Dasein, an indicator of the level and form of what is meant by history to this concrete Dasein itself. The characterization of relation is in our case – not always – especially instructive. In as much as the relation itself is always 'had' in *enactment*, the prospect is opened to grasp in a phenomenologically even more concrete way the sense-complexes in question which are designated by 'history' by bringing in the *articulation of enactment* and to carry out the *phenomenological characterization of origin* by bringing in all sense directions of the sense-complex. How far that can and must happen in the present case is determined by the task within which we were led to the necessity of a phenomenological destruction of the phenomenon of history.

§ 9 The role of the historical within the a priori tendency of philosophy

In the problem of the a priori, the absolute validity of values, respectively of the ideas of reason of the a priori, stands opposed to the relative, changeable being of the empirical and factual. The problem of the a priori is not everywhere posed in the same sense today, although philosophy sees in it its proper object, provided that it did not remain at the level of a discipline of natural science or on the plane of a purely intellectual-historical observation of types. A certain common trait can be established with regard to all considerations of the a priori. Indeed, for us it is simply important to understand the proper tendency to the a priori, irrespective of the changing points of departure and methods. The tendency to the a priori does not merely seek to secure the latter in its unique subsistence that transcends everything historical. Rather, what is to be gained by attaining the a priori is that which gives the historical and the empirical its sense, prescribes its norms, as well as that to which the historical itself is subordinate, which it serves and to which it aspires. These two moments of the a priori (whether accessory or constitutive), namely, the transcending of the empirically historical, respectively, the *supra-validity* over it as well as the *validation* of [*Hingeltung auf*] it, ultimately guide the endeavour of philosophizing and determine the concept of philosophy. (Connected with this are the moments of determination: (formally) 1. universal consideration, 2. generally valid knowledge; (in terms of content) 'riddle of life itself' – in general, supplying of the guiding norms for concrete applicability.[1])

DESTRUCTION OF THE PROBLEM OF THE A PRIORI

We now have to assess how within this a priori tendency of philosophy the role of the historical is posited and receives a solid determination. Then we have to decide how this formulation of the historical relates to the sense-complexes that were pointed out. On the latter will depend how far the problem of the historical receives its due in connection with the problem of the a priori, and to what degree the latter is itself radically determined, finally which concrete new problems arise from this – from the unsettling of the tendency of philosophy thereby motivated.

The close linking of the a priori with consciousness in Kant initially still had an effect in the revivification of philosophy in the last third of the 19th century in the sense of a neo-Kantianism, namely insofar as the a priori domains were attained along the guideline of the three basic directions or basic activities of consciousness (thinking, willing, feeling: logical, ethical, aesthetic value in Windelband, similarly with the corresponding modifications in the Marburg School). Rickert in this respect has already expressly moved away from Windelband, in fact, he finds this starting point for attaining the a priori unfruitful for two fundamental reasons. First, it is not at all possible to deduce such a thing as values from a being – here from the psychical, factual being of evaluations. Even if this was possible – Rickert thinks it impossible because of a very specific concept of psychology that appears only in his theory but nowhere else – this basis would have to be regarded as much too limited. It is indisputable that 'philosophy [needs] a factual material in order to *find* in it the manifoldness of the values'. That which claims to be valid can only be known from history.[2] *The latter* prescribes that which becomes a problem in philosophy. In history can be found the cultural goods created in historical development and to which the values are attached. Philosophy has to investigate what this claimed validity of value [*Wertgeltung*] can mean and in which sense it justifiably exists, namely as a supra-historical one. At the same time philosophy has to systematically classify these valid values. The starting point is the historical factuality of created figurations laden with values, the factuality of value statements [*Wertstellungnahmen*], the correlation of the valid value and the valuating subject.[3] Philosophy receives from epistemology (acts of recognizing, respectively of judging – recognition of an ought, of value) the authority to posit a supra-historical value content and in this sense to work on the problem of values and validity of value. As a result, philosophy is science of value. Every denial of the ought cancels itself out. In epistemological doubt, the necessity of a recognition of the ought and thereby of the valid value becomes evident. In this way, the validity of value is secured in the theoretical domain. The same can be shown analogously in the other value domains. In the formation of philosophical concepts of value their applicability to (validation of) the historical reality, which is 'a singular individual process',[4] and, ultimately, the applicability to the human being who is an historical individual and not the instance of a genus, must be taken into consideration. Its individuality lies in the quintessence of what this and exactly this individual 'has achieved with respect to the general cultural values'.[5] The human being enacts its achievements with respect to the values and is itself only from there determinable as an historical individual in its proper being-human.

In Simmel, the same thoughts attain a more animated aspect insofar as he integrates them into Bergson's metaphysics of life that he adopted almost in its entirety. The unitary concrete dynamic of organic (vital) life already generates in itself 'pre-forms' of ideal figurations. In the loss of the concrete dynamic of the life process, 'the great turn occurs'.[6] This occurrence of the 'turn towards the idea', the axial turning of life, is meant as an historical process.[7] Simmel concedes that it exceeds our capacities to pursue this process everywhere and to discover the point of the turnabout.[8] According to him, it only concerns the principle and the inner sense of this development. The vital products and functions become material contents and ideas subsisting on their own that as 'dominant features', sprung from life, now guide life itself and have a logic according to their own laws, independent of being produced and being borne by vital life. With this turnabout from the vital form to the ideal one, the human being is released from the organically vital expediency and has become free. Where the vital products of life become 'dominant features' of life itself as ideal forms, culture arises. And the 'incalculability of the culture process'[9] consists in the fact that life itself again overcomes these 'exposed' forms and makes them disappear in an objectification and something higher. At the same time metaphysical life can be determined from there. Life is always more-life and, as more-life, it is always 'more-than-life'. In this more-than-life or that more-than-life *is* life, the immanent transcendence of life, as producing (vital, organic) as well as creative spiritual life.

Similarly, Scheler defines: The human being as living being and spiritual being [*Geistwesen*] is the locus of the flaring-up of a supra-biological order, the point of breakthrough for the absolute being of the world and of values. The human being receives its unity through that which it *ought to* be and become.

Guided by the a priori and receiving its norms from it, the historically human happening, the singular process, stands in the service of the a priori. The dynamic of life forms itself within itself upwards towards something ideal. The human being as historical is the locus, the point of breakthrough of the ideal. In it itself, its factuality, in its occurring and becoming, the continuous turning [*Umwendung*] to the idea takes its course; and in this turning itself and under the norm of the idea, human life at once enacts itself. With respect to values the human being achieves, lives and creates culture and with respect to values its historical individuality, its Dasein becomes determinable.

Up to today, the a priori has been most purely and clearly elaborated in the theoretical; even more, precisely by way of this elaboration (epistemologically), both the justification and necessity of philosophy as a consideration of the a priori were actually simultaneously proved. At the same time, the theoretical a priori – despite all explicit rejection of a possible application of it to other domains – has remained formally guiding for the entire a priori problematic of philosophy. It holds the position of what is fundamental in it, such that in this guiding preconception of the a priori – for which Plato in various modifications and interpretations has always remained direction giving – the meaning and role of the historical is also determined. The model Platonic form [*Gestalt*] of the problem of the a priori did not even undergo a radical revision when the historical in its peculiarity stepped into philosophy's field of vision. It is rather that the manner of the consideration of the a priori also rubbed off on the manner of consideration and positing of the historical 'with respect to' the a priori. The a priori stands opposed to the changeable, the historical process as the coming-to-be and passing-away in time. Human beings themselves stand in this process as historical individuals; they are mere transitory occurrences, although not instances of a genus, still something factual in a process of occurring with respect to the human being achieving culture. The human being is that 'with respect to which'. Insofar as it stands within the continuously progressing process of the creation of culture the values are validated. With regard to the constantly onflooding life, ideas and ideal forms have exposited themselves in this life – as something that constantly transcends itself. Life and process are seen in an objectified way: as occurring in time. However, the a-temporality of the a priori stands opposed to the temporality of the occurring, an opposition that one is accustomed to readily make to oneself and always clearly in factical cognitive comportment: Judging is empirically factual, the judged true proposition in contrast is valid; i.e. stands beyond becoming and change. (This is even more vacuous and nonsensical than when I say: The elliptical functions stand 'beyond' the Kapp Putsch!) The supra-temporality of the ideal is therefore set in opposition to the 'temporality' of objective occurring into which the historical also fits.

Two areas sharply set off from one another thus emerge time and again. From them it then becomes a problem how they actually hang together and how the participation of the empirical, transient and historical is to be comprehended in the ideally a prioric. Right where this question of the μέθεξις is being touched on, it shows itself how the two areas basically are merely formally and abstractly generally characterized as being and being valid, as sensible and non-sensible (transcendentally turned: content and form), so that the interpretations of the 'participation' must then turn out to be just as empty and artificial.

If we now see which of the previously mentioned sense-complexes that we were referred to by the word 'history' is a possible match here in this opposition, then it is without question the one mentioned in the second place. And provided that we pay attention to the sense of relation belonging to it, it turns out that the latter entirely fits into the style and the basic attitude of the consideration of the a priori. We said: what is meant there by history is, with regard to its being an object, the correlate of a theoretically idealizing and abstract determination that disregards every concrete present. Exactly in this theoretical formulation the historical – the becoming – is, in the context of the problem of the a priori, opposed to the supra-historical a priori.

With this it becomes evident that the sense-complex of history is, within the problem of the a priori, not one which like those mentioned in III., IV. and especially V. has a peculiar relationship to concrete Dasein. In as much as among the sense-complexes III. to V., the V. displayed an especially pronounced intertwining with human Dasein, the one that was discussed in II. and functions in the problem of the a priori stands furthest removed from concrete Dasein.

Let us assume that what has been said so far is understood and it is also kept in mind that it is exactly the innermost tendency of philosophy's consideration of the a priori to attain with the a priori – despite all the preservation of purity of its in-itself-character ultimately somehow worldview like in the good sense – the norms and goals with regard to *human* life. Then it must appear astonishing that within this tendency of the a priori problematic, which is not being thought and treated independently from the mentioned opposition, exactly that concept of history is guiding which is quite inappropriate for the philosophical basic tendency and is remote from it.

It thus turns out that this a priori problematic in its ownmost tendency runs counter to itself. It is only suggested here that the philosophical systematics and system formation – both as regulating, i.e. as placing the results into a framework and as an implicitly elaborated inner systematics of the subject matter that guides the problematic – is always determined from what is fundamental and from the a prioric, that concomitantly also the systematics and system formation is always affected as well by the fundamental contrary course of the tendencies within the problem of the a priori. In this way, e.g. in Simmel, the determination of the concept of life is attained from this opposition. (The recourse to the 'open system' points to an emergency exit which has the peculiar characteristic of leading directly back into the endangered 'enclosure'.)

If we bear in mind that the consideration of the sense-complex is not yet complete, that the characterization of the sense of enactment is still pending, then the possibility arises to still more sharply illuminate in the latter the inner inappropriateness of the a priori problematic, insofar as it thereby turns out that the consideration in which history functions here is not the philosophically primordial one but one derived in a theorizing and objectifying way that has left behind concrete Dasein and the relation to it.

§ 10 Characterization of enactment: the articulation of the sense-complexes according to the sense of enactment

(a) The task of phenomenological dijudication

Right away, we direct the consideration of the sense of enactment in such a way that what is important in the present context comes forward. To gain an understanding one must recall what was said about the phenomenological destruction (cf. p. 21 ff.). The reduction to the genuine sense-complexes and the articulation of the genuine sense directions comprised in them is what is final in the phenomenological task. However, the sense-complex (e.g.) of history not only requires, according to its what-content, an understanding in the broader genetic context with

CHARACTERIZATION OF ENACTMENT

others, but the critical destruction itself, as it were, issues into what may be called the *phenomenological dijudication*. (The Latin term is selected in order to have it correspond to destruction.) This dijudication is the decision about the genealogical position which, seen from the origin, is assigned to the sense-complex. The scope and type of validity as well as the form of evidence and conditions of evidence of such dijudication is left undiscussed for now. Formally, it must be said that this decision always requires a criterion (measure). In our concrete question of the *characterization of enactment*, a criterion must be provided compared to which the enactment can be characterized as primordial or non-primordial; in fact, this can now only be carried out by way of formally indicating and in the necessarily limited way of achievement of the formally indicating.

The criterion can obviously not be taken from the outside but must co-result from the ultimate tendencies of the phenomenological problematic itself. In as much as it is a destructive and dijudicative understanding of the origin, the criterion is definitely motivated in what is concretely understood as the sphere of the origin, now worldly [?] speaking: self-worldly Dasein. What results from this in relation to enactments is the following:

An enactment is primordial if, as enactment of a relation that is at least co-directed in a genuinely self-worldly way, it requires, according to its sense, an always actual renewal in a self-worldly Dasein. It does so precisely in such a way that this renewal and the 'necessity' (requirement) of renewal inherent in it co-constitutes self-worldly existence.

That which is in contrast non-primordial, which is 'deduced', 'derived' according to a particular understanding, however, still shows within itself multifarious decisive differences. We now pursue the phenomenological dijudication of the genuine enactments of the meaning-complexes in question.

(b) The phenomenological dijudication of the genuine enactments of the meaning-complexes in question

ad I

The enactment of the relations pre-delineated in the theoretical attitudinal complex (science of history) is obviously such that it does

DESTRUCTION OF THE PROBLEM OF THE A PRIORI

not require an actual renewal in a self-worldly Dasein in the sense that it co-constitutes self-worldly Dasein. Likewise, it is not an enactment of a self-worldly also only co-directed relation in the sense that in the enactment of the relation as such the own concrete Dasein is in some way concurrently had [*mitgehabt*].

One is tempted to contest both for good reasons. The sense of relation of the theoretical attitudinal complex tends towards a domain of subject matter – it is e.g. the research or attainment of scientifically historical knowledge of a particular period of political, intellectual or religious history. In the attitudinal complex of e.g. geometry or mineralogy, there is also the direction towards a domain of subject matter; the genuine theoretical relation to it is in no way self-worldly directed. On the contrary, it is exactly the immanent requirement of this relation to keep itself free from every self-worldly directed tendency. Certainly, also here the relation as an actual one is enacted in an actual subject, such that the latter is only relevant *to that extent* which is marked off by the theoretical task of gaining knowledge itself. Availabilities, experiences and viewpoints concern actual Dasein only in its theoretically tended situation.

It is possible and factically also mostly the case that an actual self is perhaps inwardly strongly interested and involved in its theoretical tasks of this sort, however, all that does not enter into the theoretical relation as such, does not determine its sense with regard to content. The enactment is therefore not one of a self-worldly even co-directed relation. We now speak of theoretical attitudinal complexes, characterized as sciences and scientific disciplines like geometry or mineralogy. Is what has been said also valid for the attitudinal complex that is in question here? Or does one have to be wary of such transferences and understand every attitudinal complex from out of itself? Science of history also strives for objective knowledge of subject matter and is supposed to be free from 'subjective', evaluating statements; it is supposed to simply say 'how it was'. Let us take a concrete task: the attainment of historical knowledge about the Reformation and primarily about the figure of Luther, i.e. how each of them was. What was there – in the actual understanding? One can phrase it: the spiritually religious development of Luther. It becomes apprehensible, one says further, in historical understanding; and how it was will be experienced in the most immediate way only by a religious, and more exactly, a Protestant human being and historian. The objectivity, the pure apprehension of what and how it was does not depend on how many people and historians are capable of reconstructing the figure of Luther. The validity of a knowledge is not founded in the factical accessibility for several people or for a general public. However, at the same time still something is granted with this which is of importance for our context. In this theoretical, historical-understanding relation of apprehension the self-worldly Dasein of someone who is theoretical-scientifically attuned still plays an entirely different role than in the previously mentioned cases. Is not their own religiousness somehow exactly adopted here in the sense of relation, provided that understanding proceeds from one's own actual religious Dasein? Are the availabilities that also support the understanding exactly those of ownmost Dasein, that is those that concern the historically apprehending subject not only, as in the cases mentioned earlier, in its theoretically tended situation, so that the enactment would after all be an enactment of a relation which is at least co-directed in a self-worldly way? One easily sees that this is not the case. It may be the case that experiences – and those that even touch on the innermost self – also support historical understanding in a certain way that is still to be defined, the knowing subject may therefore in a certain sense and differently than in the cases above be involved with its abundance of experience. Still, the apprehending, epistemic understanding objectifying relation does not contain anything of that in itself in such a way that this relation, according to its genuine sense of relation, would be in any way co-directed towards this actual Dasein as such. This makes it necessary to mention it as a theoretical one in the context of other relations that are not to be discussed here. (The relation here is not self-worldly *co-directed* but rather in a certain way takes up what is self-worldly into the motivation; the self-worldly motivations 'are also there', but they are *free from existence* [*existenzfrei*].)

In any case, one of the moments required for the characterization as 'primordial' is missing in the enactment under discussion. Already because of this the decision about the I. meaning-complex could be made. But we will also discuss the presence [*Vorhandensein*] respectively the non-presence [*Nichtvorfindlichsein*] of the other characteristic moment, if only in order to understand more concretely by means of this discussion what was merely formally indicated by the criterion proposition just examined.

A primordial enactment is supposed to require an actual renewal in a self-worldly Dasein as such, such that this renewal in fact co-constitutes self-worldly existence.

At first one does not quite see how this moment should be at all distinguishing for an enactment, since after all every enactment is in a self-worldly Dasein. Furthermore one will say that exactly the enactment of an attitudinal complex like the one under discussion is in need of the actual renewal also for an individual self-worldly Dasein. It should not be disputed that the enactment of this attitudinal complex is in need of a repeated going-through already for the genuine appropriation in a self-worldly Dasein.

The question is, however, whether that is an actual renewal of the kind that with it a self-worldly Dasein becomes and can become existent at all. For what does this appropriation, attained and provided in such renewal, mean other than that with this the self-worldly Dasein is put in the position to, in secure and pure pursuit, leave itself behind and relinquish itself? The actual renewal required for this attitudinal complex in the sense of its possibility of appropriation and factical availability is not of such a kind that in it self-worldly Dasein becomes existent for itself but is rather an accumulation of the danger of a secure self-loss. In view of the task inherent in the corresponding relation itself, however, it means a securing of its pure carrying-out.

It still must be taken into account, however, and indeed in view of the difference that we just encountered, that the self-worldly Dasein, despite the pure theoretical relation being untouched, in fact still plays a different role, depending on whether we are dealing with e.g. geometry and mineralogy or the historical-biographical understanding of a historical figure and epochs of intellectual history. Likewise, it still has to be taken into account that this different role and relevance for a philosophical-phenomenological dijudication of e.g. the attainment of knowledge in the natural and human sciences may not be withheld and that the manner of losing oneself in the two groups of theoretical attitudinal complexes is a different one. This is a problem that is of fundamental importance in the phenomenology of the structural connection between historical and systematic theology.

In this context, the question could come up whether or not e.g. a figure who dedicates his life to scientific research and, let us suppose, attains the highest achievements that are accompanied by an upturn and progress of culture, whether or not such a figure precisely in this pure devotion to subject matter, where the whole of life, as it were, is a continued enactment of this scientific-theoretical attitudinal complex, becomes fully existent. This question must be negated. (To argue this in more detail would lead to the problem of a possible life-context determined by the idea of science – scientific life communities, universities, academies etc. – which does not concern us here.)

Insofar as the motivation complex of historical understanding functions in a way free from existence in the enactment, no enactment renewal ever reaches (touches) the self-worldly existence, never constitutes it. This context of renewal can wholly fill out an actual Dasein as objective historical process so that I am completely absorbed in it, but this *filling-out of actual Dasein* 'which lets itself be absorbed' is something different from the 'constituting of self-worldly existence', whereas 'constituting' itself is still employed as formally indicating [?]. The enactment which corresponds to the I. sense-complex is, therefore, not a primordial one because the relation is not one that is directed in a self-worldly way and the renewal of enactment is not of that kind that constitutes self-worldly Dasein as such.

We will discuss the sense-complex mentioned in the II. place at the end of this dijudicative consideration because indeed it only comes into consideration for the problem of the a priori as we encounter it.

ad III

Already when the characterization of enactment was not yet the proper task one could point to the fact that the sense-complexes mentioned in III., IV. and V. must be assigned a looser relationship to actual Dasein. In case III., we emphasized history as a people's own past, to be precise, as correlate of a preserving and of a continually newly taking over and taking along in one's own Dasein. The sense of enactment corresponding to this relation of the preserving newly taking along of one's own past in one's own actual Dasein is such that it requires renewal, in as much as that tradition is only continually preserved in continuous cultivation, whereas the latter does not need to be purposefully organized, in a detached way, in which case it already becomes un-genuine. Is, however, the tradition-preserving and tradition-forming cultivation under consideration here a renewal of enactment that *co-constitutes* actual Dasein itself? Here a concrete phenomenon is under consideration that in one respect is suited to more closely determine the sense of 'co-constituting actual Dasein'.

Also this *pervading* of actual Dasein, which holds for the preserving, that takes along, its so-called *own* past does not constitute self-worldly existence. However, in distinction to I.: the relation does not concern a

DESTRUCTION OF THE PROBLEM OF THE A PRIORI

delimited theoretical domain of subject matter and does not include in itself the pushing back of actual Dasein that is given with the *theoretical* attitude as such. The fact that Dasein co-motivates the latter itself, that it plays a role in it and determines the manner of its course co-constitutes actual Dasein. The past is there as an environing world and thus also relates back to itself as self-worldly, in as much as the self-world is experienced in and through *meaningfulness*.

The people's own past means here its deeds, achievements, customs, destinies and, indeed, in the way in which they manifest themselves in what happened earlier with that people. Such a past is preserved, upheld and cultivated by a history-'having' people, not just merely recounted, taught or handed down in the sense of a knowledge and having-knowledge about it, but rather in such a manner that the character of being known [*Gewußtheitscharakter*], which is possibly also co-given, in which this past is had, does not have its proper dominant place, but is merely subserviently subject to the dominant character of givenness. The latter is equal to that of the environing and with-world and motivates actual present Dasein in the manner of such instances of meaningfulness; it is concurrently there in the ambit of the concrete situation of actual Dasein and plays a determining role in it. In this sense of concurrently-being-there, of concurrently-playing-a-role, of concurrently-occurring in the factical world of experience, the past (respectively its continuous renewal according to tradition) *co*-constitutes actual Dasein. This secondary co-constituting of actual Dasein is, however, not that which is meant in the just mentioned criterion of origin. That becomes clear if we consider the context that is taken into account in relationship to a people (a community) with respect to a proper self-worldly personal Dasein. In doing so, we take into account only the person's own history, namely, in the sense of how the word is meant in our present context. The past achievements, also the failed attempts and the mis-achievements, further encounters, events as well as conventions can also play a role – and yet they do not constitute self-worldly existence itself. This is not an accumulation of pasts that stretch into the future, in as much as actual Dasein is understood as self-worldly existence. Both concepts will later be determined more sharply. The human being can *be there* [*da sein*], have Dasein, without existing. In as much as it exists, everything that is concurrently there in the hitherto characterized sense, which concurrently plays a role in the character of factical life-*meaningfulness*, is intensified [*zugespitzt*] towards a dominating – (what does 'dominating' mean – in the existentiell enactment?) – mode of meaningfulness with the direction towards the self-world. This mode of meaningfulness is that of the continued *impetus* to the self-worldly directed destruction. (From there the properly decisive critique of Bergson is to be initiated!)

The renewal of the past, however, as it is intended in case III. both with regard to the community and a self-world, does not co-constitute self-worldly existence but rather holds actual Dasein precisely in a constant pushing away from this possibility, precisely holds it firmly to environing and with-worldly instances of meaningfulness; self-worldly ones are not there in their existentiell character but merely concurrently play a role like environing worldly ones. The enactment of the relation mentioned in III. does have a mode of renewal but it is not of such a kind that it co-constitutes self-worldly existence.

Also about the second moment of the criterion of origin we can now discern something with regard to the enactment under discussion. The enactment must belong to a relation that is at least *co*-directed in a self-worldly way.

At first glance, also this moment appears here to be present like that of renewal, in as much as the relatedness to the past, the relation to it co-indicates, co-includes the pointing back to actual Dasein, however – as is easy to see – not directed to self-worldly existence, but to self-worldly instances of meaningfulness, provided that they are released from existence and merely concurrently play a role in what concerns the environing world, e.g. *my* lecture in the context of the university business or even of *my* work. (Here we hit on a typical relation, as far as it is a pre- and mixed form of such ones that in themselves have sense-of-relation-like 'repercussion'.)

In this way, the enactment turns out to be non-primordial, by which it itself is not yet primordially understood, even if we also consider the brief positive characterization.

ad IV

In the IV. place, we treated *history* in the sense of a past that is not one's own, provided that, however, it is accentuated through actual, *not* specifically self-worldly directed (environing world-)tendencies of Dasein and is 'had' in the manner of the being familiar which takes guidance from it.

Here it already becomes apparent that the moment of the self-worldly directed relation drops out, so that, primordiality is actually out of the question.

Contrariwise, to the relation of the being familiar, namely of that which takes guidance, enactmentally belongs a mode of renewal that itself is motivated in actual, but environing worldly directed tendencies of Dasein. Again, this enactment concurrently plays a role, namely in the ambit of the situation (horizon) pre-delineated by the tendencies of Dasein.

Provided that in case III., along with a mode of renewal, a being co-directed to actual Dasein can be encountered also in the relation, even if not existentielly self-worldly, the enactment in question is closer to the primordial. 'Closer' here is meant neither spatially nor in the meaning of psychical intensity, rather the meaning becomes understandable only in the preconception and re-conception of what is itself primordial.

ad V

In case V. there is a sense of enactment that comes even closer to the primordial, so that here past is had as the ownmost one and this having, in fact, enacts itself in such a way that the ownmost past also loses the environing worldly character into which the self-worldly instances of meaningfulness constantly fall back: *falling-away* of a purely self-worldly directed meaningfulness into the environing worldly one and there into the faded layer of what is mostly secondarily carried along. Case V. is situated closest to the primordial – and still is not the primordial itself – *pure* self-worldly meaningfulness. The enactment is in each case and necessarily such that what has been self-worldly meaningful *arises* again in it; not in such a way that I would transport myself back into earlier situations or that I would feign that I lived something earlier again, rather I seize my own past so that it again and again is had for the first time and that I myself am always affected anew by myself and 'am' in renewed enactment. This 'like for the first time' undergoes even closer determinations; first, that it is entirely unrelated to the environing world and then that it does not mean a first-time appearing and occurring in an individual stream of consciousness, in this sense, it would occur and occurs in its necessary renewal never again for the first but for the second, third etc. time. This moment of 'like for the first time' that lies in the sense of enactment does not lose itself in the renewal, does not wear itself out but becomes with it itself always more surprising. The self-affectedness 'grows' in a particular sense and every 'like for the first time' is characterized as precursor: *the rejection of every trace of finality*. (It is not a latent being familiar or a habit that could arise as the 'result' of this renewal; it is precisely of such a nature that it blocks the way for any formation of habit. The habitual is self-worldly meaningful, but not constitutive of existence. The instances of meaningfulness of life experience – environing world, with-world, self-world – and above all precisely the self-worldly ones in the mode of 'being intensified'.)

The sense of enactment appears here as already richly articulated according to its mode of renewal and at the same time as one that belongs to self-worldly directed relations. The moments of origin seem to be fulfilled here and therewith the dijudication on primordiality seems unmistakable and final. Exactly this appearance of the formally indicating consideration, which feigns finality and universal applicability, makes a fool of philosophy when the latter believes to find itself and its task, which is as such meagre and therefore so hard to detect and establish, in abstract systematic conceptualization.

Within philosophy, the formal indication has an indispensible meaning that can be made understood, however, only if the formal indication and that which is indicated by it is not hypostasized and made into the goal and object of philosophical consideration, but stands in a firmly definite way in the service of the task of philosophy: of the primordial understanding that makes aware, i.e. is at the same time genuinely motivated from the concrete and factical, not as that which is common to the factical but as not prejudging, however, neither decisively achieving, pre-delineating touching on the factical.

ad VI

The characterization of enactment for case VI. is of importance with respect to the phenomenological understanding of factical life experience. In as much as it always falls away from its origin and fades in its content, relations like the one mentioned in VI. are *always non-primordial*. The *renewal* that comes into consideration here – as custom, practice, convention [*Sitte*] – is not a kind of the primordial but has an entirely different relation to it.

ad II

The II. sense-complex that is present in the a priori problem is determined as the objective totality of the being of what occurs. As a possible relation

DESTRUCTION OF THE PROBLEM OF THE A PRIORI

we found a consideration, encompassing the totality, from the side of an ideal subject which as absolute observer stands opposed to the occurring and constantly has the latter available at once. The relation is directed purely towards the subject matter, towards the object; and even if it were co-directed towards the subject, it would touch on one that is not an actually concrete matter but – as we have already seen – an idealized, abstractive one, in fact, in a particular sense; abstract idealization of a concrete self-world, as far as it is attuned in a theoretically observing way, that is of an enactmental complex that already in itself, as we saw in I., leaves behind actual self-worldly Dasein in the sense of the existing one. This enactmental complex whose mode of renewal pushes away self-worldly Dasein is in II. a merely thought and idealized one that is not at all concretely actual. Provided that one takes into account the character of enactment, which is assigned to this idealizing abstraction, this character of enactment proves again to be a theoretical one to which what we just said applies, so that therefore that which in II. is meant by history is correlate of an exponentially theoretical relational enactment. With those enactmental complexes something is given which so little co-constitutes self-worldly existence that instead existence is simply demolished. That is required by the content of the sense-complex, that is, by that which in the problem of the a priori stands opposed to the a priori, towards which the latter aims and which it transcends in a norm-giving way, while after all the consideration of the a priori in its actual tendency aspires to be set in motion with respect to the concrete-factical human being. The sense of history posited in the problem of the a priori persists precisely at the cost of explicitly pushing away that towards which the problem itself is aimed. That towards which the problem tends precisely does not let the posing of the problem emerge at all. That is: the human being in its concrete, individual historical Dasein.

PART TWO

On the destruction of the problem of lived experience

§ 11 The transition to the second problem group and the relation between psychology and philosophy

In the course of the previous considerations distinctions were encountered such as: concrete historical Dasein, actually self-worldly Dasein, self-worldly existence, which points to the fact that – even if the concrete human being was posited in the problem of the a priori – only a starting point for the problematic would be attained. At the same time it is now still conceded that generally the a priori tendency is a meaningful one.

Up to now two things have been attained: 1. The problematic of the a priori is shown in its innermost core as running counter to itself. 2. With this we are at the same time positioned in a perspective on concrete primordial existence (speaking objectively from the outside: the primordially factical, the primordial facticity). *The preconception is indicated.*

It was already said earlier (p. 17f.): Even though philosophy ultimately aims at the a priori – the principles of reason and the norm-giving values – a co-considering of the spirit's directions of shaping and creating that are assigned to those principles and receive their normativity from them is nevertheless unavoidable.

Therefore, however much the concrete human being seems to disappear from the problem of the a priori and the ultimate objecthood of philosophy, the human being is in another respect the object of rich and multiform philosophical considerations. Everything that in the broadest sense is called psychology, but also logic, ethics, and aesthetics

DESTRUCTION OF THE PROBLEM OF LIVED EXPERIENCE

strives in this direction. 'Activities', 'capacities', 'functions' and 'attitudes' of the human spirit have since time immemorial been one of the objects of philosophy. It is well known what Plato, Aristotle and above all the Stoics have brought to light in this regard.

Let us see how and in which sense and to what extent the human being as such is an object of philosophy: the human being as something achieving, creating, experiencing life – *life as manifoldness of lived experience*. We have limited the II. problem group characterized in this way to one specific problem, namely, in which way life as living experience becomes rationally accessible for philosophy. Provided that living experience in its totality is today posited as irrational, it is the problem of rationally coming to terms with the irrational. That looks like a specifically epistemological problem, applied to philosophy itself (that is, logic of philosophy or epistemology of philosophy). It should, however, not be understood in the sense that we are asking in the first place about limits, scope as well as degree of certainty and mode of grounding or 'logical structure' of such knowledge of lived experience. The treatment of the problem of irrationality has more fundamental goals so that in the end it turns out that the problem in question is not an isolated remote, secondary one.

Also here, the way of proceeding is again the destruction, to be precise, guided *by the same preconception*. The problem of irrationality is only an especially emphasized specification for the pursuit of the directions in which the human being as experiencing [*erlebender und erfahrender*] is an object of philosophical knowledge. That means: here we are pre-given – which becomes understandable from the character of the entire problem group – certain relations as more or less highlighted[1] and search for their genuine sense-complexes, which themselves, under the guidance of the preconception, are subjected to the destructive and dijudicative understanding of the origin.

Without this preconception and the fundamental experience that motivates it, having for their part already been explicitly considered, it is first of all indicated by the characterization of enactment in the I. problem group that everything intensifies in a certain, not yet definitely determined way towards the concrete actual, existing self-world. We ask in which way, to what extent and in which basic orientation the self-world is theoretically apprehended and objectified in different typical philosophies and how far this theoretical tendency – analogous to the question in the problem of the a priori – fits into what philosophy fundamentally always strives for. Furthermore we ask how the a priori motive, the history motive, the consciousness-subject-lived experience motive and the worldview motive, respectively the motive of universal consideration, hang together and whether a concrete sphere of the origin can be found.

The complex of questions that crops up here could at first and following contemporary efforts be connected with the problem of psychology. Although psychology necessarily has a part in the following considerations, namely psychology in the most differing meanings, our question does not pertain to the theory of science, about psychology as science: the question about its domain of subject matter, about the elaboration of the latter out of a genuine world of experience, the highlighting of this world in a fundamental experience from factical life experience.

Our questioning is not limited to psychology; it is searching for the origin as such out of which any theory of science and therefore also the science of psychology receives its pre-delineations. It thereby turns out that psychology has a closer relation to philosophy, which is always concealed in a classification of the sciences. From out of this closer relation of psychology to philosophy it becomes understandable if in the destructive regress one comes from it into the self-worldly domain without any detours.

As much as we drop the explicit limitation to psychology it still becomes necessary – exactly because the borders are still mixed up – to draw on this limitation in what follows. Instead of too narrow a consideration of psychology as it pertains to the theory of science, the following could be treated under the title 'self-reflection'. These remarks are not concerned with a question of title and designation but seek to indicate directions of consideration and therewith provide understanding as to *which one* will be concretely pursued. But, even in this sense, the problem would be too narrow and would prejudge too much with the title reflection; as if it were about the turning back on oneself and this in the manner of reflecting, pondering, of the theoretically thoughtful [*denkmäßigen*] consideration.

After all, the problem of irrationality even in this formulation has its source in a certain contemporary comprehension. We take only as a first instruction, which may not misguide, for the least possible prejudicial posing of the problems: *how living experience is had.*

Before certain guiding sense-complexes are singled out, we attempt a general orientation – or rather disorientation – with reference to the various and intersecting series of problems within which our question – and again in various manners and in graduated importance – plays a role.

In addition to the confusion regarding subject matter, one furthermore has to struggle with a bewildering terminology, which presumably reaches the maximum of what can be achieved at all in this domain in the problem sphere under discussion. The reason for this is again one of subject matter, namely the abundance of the problematic and the many kinds of possible approach.

There is indeed a lot of talk about the problem-historical treatment of the history of philosophy, and precisely in view of the contemporary problem situation it would be an urgent task to investigate how the problem of psychology as science is in each case guided by the dominant theoretical basic motives. However, in this way the question is not final, the decisive one is still to come, namely *whether* the access to the mental may *at all* be rightly determined already at the very outset from out of any kind of theoretical determination of the task, even if completely unconsciously and inexplicitly or whether the phenomenological destruction does not actually have to begin exactly just here and not only within various theoretical attempts at the objectification of mental life. Within the phenomenological destruction seen in this way, we run into the same difficulty which in the end disfigures the problem of the a priori in its core. There is the necessity of a fundamental confrontation with Greek philosophy and its disfiguration of Christian existence. The *true idea of Christian philosophy*; Christian not a label for a bad and epigonal Greek one. The way to a primordial Christian – Greek-free [*griechentumfreien*] – theology.

SECTION ONE
The destructing consideration of the Natorpian position

§ 12 The four viewpoints of destruction

The problem of irrationality is, as we have seen, posited as the guiding problem for the destruction of the II. problem group – the question in which manner living experience is philosophically had, the question about the relation of apprehension directed towards living experience.

The ambiguity that exists with regard to the concept of lived experience as such is increased by the fact that living experience is always thought as related, to be precise, *as* related to an experiencing 'I', subject or consciousness, so that the ambiguity of these concepts entwines itself in the most diverse variations with the first mentioned ambiguity. Thus for the destruction it is pre-given: relations of apprehension as directed to living experience *and* the experiencing subject; they show how the 'I' and its living experience – what we indicate with *self-world* – is philosophically apprehended and had.

With regard to the destruction and the dijudication of the relations of apprehension pre-given as 'cases' from the history of philosophy that are available to us in an historically objectified way, each time several things are therefore to be kept in mind. For facilitation of understanding this should be indicated in advance. For the *destruction* we take into consideration:

1. how living experience as such is had
2. how in this having the character of unity and manifoldness of the complex of lived experience is meant

DESTRUCTING CONSIDERATION OF THE NATORPIAN POSITION

3. how the 'I' relates to this or within this complex determined by the character of unity and manifoldness
4. how the 'I' itself is experienced.

Consequently, the aim is the attainment of a decision about which preconception is guiding for the philosophical tendency of apprehension and to what extent it is *explicitly* brought into relief from a pre-theoretical primordial fundamental experience and to what extent it is not, but is rather transferred and exceeded in being made to conform to already available theoretical forms of relations of apprehension.

In this, for now only the *relation* of apprehension is taken into account and the characterization of enactment is entirely deferred because the latter is mostly either not at all or merely of casual secondary interest and one understandably avoids including it somehow in the determination of the concept of philosophy; this is because of an unconscious prejudice suggested by the sciences that are indifferent to enactment, which is explicitly sanctioned by philosophy.

If we further take into account that for the full carrying through of *this* destruction with regard to our guiding goal, the first problem group must also be taken into account at the same time and the questions become increasingly complicated, it is appropriate to present and communicate this problem group a bit differently, namely in a way in which not for every individual step all the cases to be subjected to destruction are always brought in at the same time, are pursued in their entirety from level to level, but rather each for itself. The 'examples' – I still speak in this way because the sense of such facticities is yet to be laid down – for the relations of apprehension to be destructed are taken, for already intimated reasons, from the living present, in fact they are chosen in such a way that decisive positions are thereby destructed. These positions that belong to the present and dominate contemporary philosophizing are for their part historically conditioned so that it is appropriate to briefly point to the often noted particular character of modern philosophy and from the beginning keep the subsequent destruction free from gross misunderstandings.

Usually the turn to modern philosophy is characterized with Descartes, with reference to the fact that already in the Renaissance the independence of thinking with regard to belief, dogmas and theology took shape and the predominance of Aristotelianism was shaken and in this way the liberation from the scholasticism of the Middle Ages was in the offing, although it should be pointed out that the predominance of Aristotle in the Middle Ages merely exists in the heads of those who know the Middle Ages from third- and fourth-rate compendiums; also the recently noted appearance of Platonic currents falls victim to the same procedure which comes from the outside and divides up the philosophy of the Middle Ages and the other [?] philosophies; nothing of the actual sense and spirit remains in this division.

In Descartes, one sees the purity of independent, liberated philosophical thinking and its self-grounding achieved again for the first time since Greek philosophy. It had a concrete effect in the foundation of the philosophical problematic on the *cogito ergo sum*. The 'I' or the consciousness has thus moved into the centre of the philosophical problematic and has in the following times emerged in an ever more acute and versatile way. Indeed, one believes to have accomplished a considerable and accordingly praiseworthy achievement of historical objectivity, if one admits that already Augustine had introduced the absolute evidence of self-consciousness into philosophy. One even goes so far as to call Augustine, due to this achievement, the 'first modern human being', as Windelband does. Well, he would have probably crossed himself before this compliment, which means that it is virtually the pinnacle of misunderstanding to see Augustine and his 'principle of consciousness' in this way. There, these considerations stand in an entirely different fundamental context than in Descartes for whom God plays a role merely as epistemological auxiliary saint [*Nothelfer*]. Therein lies what is wrongly called Christian philosophy, patristics and scholasticism of the Middle Ages – Luther included – a spiritual world that, from Descartes on, modern philosophy ever more sharply blocked itself off from. This blocking off reached its peak in Fichte and Hegel precisely because they spoke so much about Christianity, from where then in turn the influence of the Hegelian left on the religion-historical school becomes understandable and thus on all of modern Protestant theology as well as on Catholic theology, to the extent to which it believes to get its scientific character going by means of exact historical research.

As much as it is fundamentally unradical to philosophize today merely with regard to a preceding philosophy (Kant, Fichte or Hegel), it would be misguided to exploit a combating of philosophy as determined from Descartes on in the sense of a repristination of the Middle Ages as it in part happens today. That would indeed not be unmodern, provided that this could be relevant as a measure, since the official makers of culture

DESTRUCTING CONSIDERATION OF THE NATORPIAN POSITION

now merely keep talking and writing about the 'Gothic human being'. That is probably the highest degree of impertinence and unspiritual lack of dignity we experience today; and the fact that on the official side of the church such spiritual currents are even registered as a welcome approach and are apologetically exploited gives an idea of what one can expect to get out of the so-called Christian philosophy there.

This is being said in the sense of a destruction of a certain modern religious consciousness that can easily mislead into an un-genuine resentment against modern philosophy and into an even more un-genuine Christianity and Christian thinking. Provided that the dangerousness of this new contamination of the contemporary lifestyle, which in itself is un-genuine enough, is recognized, what follows will probably remain free of gross misunderstandings.

The 'exemplary' relations are taken from the contemporary problematic, however, as relations of apprehension in the sense of the orientation for a decision about the possible unarticulated [?] pretheoretical fundamental experience. The identification is connected to the names of their discoverers and representatives. The sequence is intentional; we consider Natorp, James, Münsterberg and Dilthey.

The destructing consideration of the Natorpian position is necessary and fruitful for multiple reasons. It is therefore placed at the beginning: 1. It stands in its tendency and according to the character of the preconception to be defined, as it were, in the most extreme opposite end with regard to the one which is supposed to be attained in these considerations. 2. As much as it is furthest removed – in our sense: far from the origin [*ursprungsfern*] and depraved – it radically and intensely searches in its sense for the 'origin'. The designation is often explicitly used terminologically. In this way arises the possibility of differentiating between two radically opposed origin-concepts and attaining a judgment about the rigour and consistency of the Natorpian consideration of the origin – more precisely reconstruction. 3. The Natorpian position is entirely in line with Fichtean and Hegelian thinking. Motives and tendencies that today are aspired to in various modifications in referring back to Fichte and Hegel are consciously brought to life. 4. The connection offers the opportunity here to make up for, and therefore supplement, the critical consideration that was planned for the previous class.

The fundamental question that dominates all that follows is the one about the manner and sense of the having of living experience (whereby having ≠ theoretical apprehension – comprehending). Simultaneously this also includes the question of how the self-world is had.

§ 13 Natorp's general reconstructive psychology

From the discussion of the problem of the a priori we know that the life-forms of achieving and creating are subordinate to ideas, values and laws of ought and are, according to the basic nature of the last mentioned, classified into logical, ethical, aesthetic and religious values. This achieving, forming and experiencing is now supposed to be experienced in a final philosophical consideration. This living experience is objectification in the direction of shaping, positing and forming. This living experience itself, as experiencing, as the 'in and for consciousness', the subjective, is now in its turn supposed to be depicted. In this depiction, the manifoldness of the objectifications is gathered together again, concretely unified. It is only in this task that philosophy attains its radical completion and foundation. This task of depicting the subjective falls to psychology, namely philosophical psychology. In the sense of the order of knowledge it is not prior, but posterior to the other disciplines. It is supposed to apprehend the 'ultimate, fulfilled reality', 'life'[1] in the full sense of its concretion; at least it has to methodologically determine and pre-delineate this task as the task of an infinite process which can never be completed: 'restoration of the entire concretion of the experienced'.[2] (For a comprehensive critique of Natorp's philosophical psychology it is to be taken into account that this general psychology – *formal* phenomenology – contains the problem: of the role of the formal, of the consideration of such distributions, of the function of such 'limit categories':[3] whether and to what extent they are grasped in the sense of the formal indication, and how the function of the *formal indication* is to be understood from out of the *fundamental task* of philosophy.[4])

(a) The method of reconstruction

What is decisive now is the clear posing of the problems for psychology. The method in which the subjective as subjective is depicted must be found. The sense of this depiction of the subjective – the subjectification – is opposed to all objectification. Natorp sees the basic mistake of all contemporary psychology in that it objectifies the subjective, i.e. apprehends it in the manner of object determination and systematizes it conceptually. (Clear consciousness of method; 'genuine apprehension', 'fundamental experience' – not parallelization to natural science or science of objects in general.) He has already in all acuity brought this misguided aim of psychology to attention in his *Introduction to Psychology According to Critical Method* (1888), formulated it more sharply and developed it in the *General Psychology* (1912), cf. *Philosophie* (1911, p. 139 ff.). Therefore the problem is the concrete complex of lived experience, the immediate character of the soul, the pure subjectivity and its genuine apprehension, its epistemic 'illumination and securing'.

What matters now is to determine this subjective more closely. What is meant by it? In which sense is the subjective spoken of? It is said for instance: this view, this comprehension, this depiction is merely 'subjective'. If I look from here at the library building, I see it from this specific side, from this and that distance, lighting and so forth. The view – taken literally – is merely subjective in contrast to one that is called *in itself*, an *objective* one. That the lectern presents itself to me in this colour is merely subjective; objectively, what was called lectern is to be determined differently. We see the moon as a disk, objectively it is determined differently. I speak of 'subjective' always with regard to something objectively determined and determinable that is anticipated [*voraus- und vorweggenommenes*]. In this way, the difference between the physical and the psychical is cleared up. The objectively physical is what is in itself objectively, scientifically, lawfully determined. The subjective – colours, sounds, i.e. contents of sensation that I am right now experiencing in this and that condition – is subjective and therefore 'set aside' by the objective determination of science. The subjective is what appears to a temporally particular subject precisely in this and that way; it is not the φαίνεσθαι ('the lived experience that something appears to me')[5] but that which appears; and in being turned towards this appearing, the objective determination *posits* the object. The objective thing is only uncovered out of the appearing. It is, as it were, a sublimate of the appearances, the X that presents itself as an A. On a new level of scientific objectification, that which was thing (object) becomes itself subjective again: the X becomes an A by virtue of a new X being posited and intended as the task of objective determination. In doing so there nevertheless always remains an identical object, an ultimate X is maintained. These levels do not designate different worlds but one and the same world, only in different levels and degrees of objective determination, of the approach to that which is in itself and absolutely objectively valid.

That which appears, the merely subjective – modern natural science unambiguously shows this – is more and more objectified. This process never stands still. What was objectively meant merely appears on a higher level. From here the sense of 'physical – psychical', 'outside and inside' can be determined. The opposition is not a fixed one; it does not designate two areas differing in terms of subject matter but is a flowing correlative one, a correlation which is itself in movement. The subjective is therefore only something subjective with regard to something objective, to be precise, *of this level*. The opposition can still be further illustrated by those of: unification and what is manifold, form and matter, relationship and what is related, what is represented and presentation.

The subject that is now 'set aside' in the progressing process of the objectification is not entirely a nothing but something 'at hand'; it is something that 'requires explanation'.

'The question about the subjective from which, indeed out of which this instance of what is objective came to be known can always be raised and is to be raised.'[6] The traversed levels – as levels of objectification – *are* and pose the task of going back to them. The objectification therefore becomes a mere means for the knowledge of the traversed subjective, but also a necessary means.

Thus the correlation exists between 'peripheral expansion' in the objectification and 'central consolidation' of the subjective that is set aside.[7]

Therefore to the extent to which the process of subjectification – more exactly its apprehension – is dependent on the objectification carried out, it will be possible for its part to set the subjectification in motion all the more securely and completely the more purely pronounced the objectification has become. The subjectification in its particular character becomes understandable all the more radically as the objectification itself (in the object of the subjectification) has developed itself.

The positing of the object is determination, establishment by law. The more general the laws and the relationships of the instances of lawfulness, the more radically objective is the determination, so that in the most abstract and ideal lawfulness the individual, that which is to be determined depicts itself most concretely and is determined most fully and truly: it is the intersection of the entirety of the sequences of ultimately abstract lawfulness that announce themselves in it.

Objectification is abstraction, separation. In the subjectification, however, the going back is to be made, the totality of the subjective that is set aside is to be apprehended as the subjective of the objective in its full correlativity and in this way the concretion of the full lived experience is to be attained.

The discretion of the fixed points of the objectification is to be transferred into the continuity of the all-round continuous transition, the correlativity. (Objectifying: probably [?] domain – stratum; subjectifying: process – stage.)

Up to now the 'psychical' was only thought 'in opposition to the "physical", that is, to the objectification in the law of nature'.[8] It was only thought as the subjective as far as it is set aside in *this* process of objectification and in its turn pre-delineates a task.

This limitation of the consideration is now to be superseded again. The 'standpoint of correlativity' is to be extended 'to the domains of will, art-forming and religion'.[9]

But even with this extension we remain 'in the same general direction of precisely the positing-of-the-object'.[10] 'Reduction to laws is the common characteristic of every kind of objectifying knowledge.'[11]

There are two fundamental kinds of law: laws of being and laws of ought. In all knowledge concerning that which is particular to culture objects, laws of being and laws of ought combine. Now, the intended known fact already has, with respect to the 'content' (appearance) that presents it, a higher level of objectivity. Now, the ought in its turn, as an even higher level of objectification, stands opposite to this being. Thereby the ought is seen with regard to lawful validity, i.e. with regard to a subsistence or being, again epistemologically. The ought, therefore, includes in itself the claim to a validity of an even higher rank. It is therefore a being that lies still beyond (ἔτι ἐπέκεινα) the being of facts. In what we last considered, the laws that determine the ought show themselves as continuously connecting to, as it were, the ones that determine being. In a certain sense only 'the restricting condition of the time elation is superseded', the 'unitary relation' of lawfulness however is held on to.[12] In this way a unitary direction of the object-relationship of objectification combines in being and ought. (In his essay in the *Kantstudien*, Natorp then goes beyond this parallelization and the persisting side by side towards a *deduction* from an ultimate logical system-ground.[13])

Also the sciences which deal with the ultimate ground layings of law, that is, logic, ethics, aesthetics and philosophy of religion, are objectifying, in fact in an even more radical sense than the concrete sciences of objects. They continue the work of objectification even further up to the ultimate abstraction. These laws that scientifically set forth the philosophical principles must relate to those of the concrete sciences of objects like 'major premises of the deduction'.[14] They unite in the idea of an ultimate logic, the logic of the origin. (The objectification and subjectification are themselves intensified and simultaneously *superseded* in the whole of philosophy. *Guiding the objectification* – ultimate lawfulness.)

Provided therefore that psychology has the task of giving the logos to the psyche, of theoretically determining the subjective, it cannot be one of the objectifying sciences, neither of the objectifying sciences of culture nor of the philosophically fundamental-methodological sciences of law.

To the extent to which one sets oneself the task – like Lipps and Husserl – of describing immediate living experience, one comports oneself objectifyingly; it is a low-level objectification, yet it is suitable to lead closer to the subjective. Description: subsumption – abstraction – quiescence [*Stillegung*],[15] i.e. not related to something objective, not in the constituting function.

The objectification is not superseded as long as this subjective is taken as its own delimited domain of subject matter instead of seeing it in its subjective character, namely as something *subjective* of something objective, *as* that which is set aside in the objectification, which nonetheless necessarily belongs to it.

The subjective of every level, that which appears, is as something numerically and generically identical first – taken in the direction of objectification – *depiction* of a law and then – in the direction of subjectification – *moment* of the subject's living experience. The depiction of the subjective is always subjectification of something objective.

The full concrete subjectivity is thus attained by subjectifyingly envisaging the entire cosmos of objectifications of being and ought. Each level of objectification corresponds to a level of subjectification. These levels must not be considered in isolation and immobilized but are to be studied in their movement and correlativity. Here an infinity opens up in subjectivity that is never reached but is there in the clearly formulated method and task of subjectification. In this way the standpoint of the 'method' now leads all the more into the abundance of life[16] that rests on *correlativity*.

In this regard, Natorp sees an ultimate lack of clarity in Kant because he does not consistently and in principle see subjectivity always 'in exact counter-relation' to objectivity.[17] Thus it happened that the subjective appears 'now as an excluding opposite of objectivity, now virtually as its ground'.[18] 'The conditions of sensibility are subjective and *therefore not* objectively valid in themselves or in the transcendental sense, the pure conditions of understanding are subjective and *therefore precisely* objectively valid [...] This is compatible only if the conditions of understanding are *ultimately valid* and the conditions of sensibility are *not ultimately valid* conditions of the knowledge of objects *on the side of the subject*.'[19] The stark dualism is to be dissolved and made flexible in the pure correlation of consciousness and object. Also the unity of consciousness is no less ultimately valid! Does not the subjectivity in this way disappear in the objectivity? Certainly: coincidence, unity of the *correlation*. The question how the two are one after all only becomes clear if the counter-relation is thought not as a resting one but '*infinite* in its flexibility'.[20]

Where is the 'transition to subjectification', 'the reinsertion into the totality of the complex of lived experience'?[21] *Turning around* – new attitude – *direction of consideration!!* Sense of direction! The subjective is not immediately known and given but must first be attained so that the process of objectification is reversed and all that is set aside is in its turn apprehended in its objectifiying accomplishment and in this accomplishment as a moment of subjectivity. The method of subjectification is that of *reconstruction*. The more purely and set apart the steps of objectification 'lay in view',[22] the more surely the reconstruction 'takes those steps, as it were, backwards again'.[23]

The objectification: 'as much as it is in a sense opposed to the task of psychology, [...] It nevertheless enacts itself without doubt in consciousness itself, as consciousness'.[24] The proof of its form therefore, its 'psychological characterization', belongs to the task of psychology.[25] But one must be wary of still expecting much from this task. The objectification complex, seen subjectively, is ultimately the 'unity of the view',[26] the 'unity of the manifold'. The latter is, however, primordial in such a way that it would be a futile effort to trace it back to something. The reference to this most immediate, to the law of lawfulnesses, the primal law of the method belongs to reconstruction.

Psychology cannot reconstruct anything that was not previously constructed. In terms of content and scope, objectification and subjectification coincide with regard to what is to be researched, only the direction is diametrically opposed. The logical (objective) always remains the opposite side of *all* that is psychical (subjective).

(b) The disposition of psychology

Now we still have to attain a concrete pre-view of the goal of philosophical psychology, which aspires to an apprehension of the totality of what is experienced, by means of 'the establishment of the natural disposition of psychological investigation'.[27] That such a disposition and its establishment is possible is by no means self-evident, especially not if psychology is merely given the task of describing individual occurrences and 'appearances' [*Auftritte*] in consciousness. That would merely lead to an external piling up and classification into groups but not to an actual 'unity of system'. All classifications of psychology reveal their descent from the objective, from that which was objectified by and in the psychical (subjective). The classifications and divisions are always attained also with regard to areas and object-domains, not merely by looking at the psychical manifold.

There is indeed no other way, it is only that the task must, if it is to be scientific, proceed on its way purely and consciously: One must proceed from the objectifications with all methodological consciousness and it must become clear that the subjective to which one tries to go back, is 'something different' than the objective, not a mere special domain of the objective. (By means of those two consciously emphasized moments Natorp's *General Psychology* seeks to differentiate itself from every other attempt at a laying of the ground.)

In the objectification-complexes, above all in the most abstract culminations, system unities are already pre-figured. Only in this way does the possibility of a psychological systematics of the subjective arise. The task at hand for general psychology now is to set up the fundamental categories of psychology.

The actually system-forming concept of psychology is that of *potency*. Understood as dynamis in opposition to the *actuality* of the objectifying positing, potency implies the *possibility* of the latter. The concept of potency is to be distinguished from the objective concept of condition in which the *conditioning* is, *in terms of content*, always different from that which it conditions, while in the concept of potency as it is here understood [?] the condition is only characterized by what it conditions. In the relation between potency and act the primal relation of the determinable to the determining and determined is expressed. Potency, of which all fundamental concepts of psychology speak, is the possibility of determination.

DESTRUCTING CONSIDERATION OF THE NATORPIAN POSITION

This primal relationship 'is now simply valid in the entire progression of levels of objectification, that is, also that of the subjectification corresponding to the latter: for each higher level of objectification the lower one means potency, for every lower one the higher one means the corresponding actualization'.[28] The regress from the objectifications, from what is actual to the possibilities, ultimately leads to a lowermost potency (πρώτη ὕλη), to the ultimate subjective bases which are prior to all determination and objectification, respectively prior to all actual positing. In actual living experience, which is always objectifying positing, something like this is not encountered; but it can be deduced 'with indubitable necessity' by means of the method.[29] This lowermost limit of consciousness is merely another expression of the 'required method itself',[30] which after all guarantees the apprehension of the concrete vitality of the totality of what is experienced. This ultimate bottom of the experienceable is to be thought in entirely undifferentiated complexity, that is, *without determination*. On this side of this lowermost limit of consciousness – the chaos out of which the totality of the (formed) world of consciousness emerges – there is only determination, division and differentiation up to the primal divisions of consciousness, whose elaboration is what matters in the disposition of psychology: fundamental kinds of the content of consciousness. 'Levels of consciousness and directions of consciousness' are two basic differentiations about which it cannot be said which precedes the other. (Here a will to system and ordering becomes apparent which arrives at a limit. And why?)

With regard to the levels of consciousness, the basic distinction in the theoretical domain is that of sensibility and thinking, which already developed early in Greek philosophy and the analogous division in the domain of striving and of feeling. The *potency* for this division is at once two sided: *Potency of separation* and *potency of conjunction*. The potency of separation comes down to 'sensation' as the ultimate terminus; and potency of conjunction which is indeed the necessary correlate for all separation: 'representation'. The resulting levels are therefore: sensation, representation and thinking, in the last of which the two-sidedness and correlativity of separation and conjunction (sensation and representation) attains clear conceptual expression, the *correlativity* of both. The individual or the separated is from now on always the separated of a conjunction or the discretion of something continuous.

The other basic differentiation bases itself on the distinction between the directions of objectification, on that between the *being and ought relationship*. The latter stands in definite connection with the levels of consciousness. The being and ought relationship can be pursued on the three levels and these levels can be inserted again into the directions of objectification.

Being means: something determined, something posited, discrete fixed point; the ought has a direction, aims at *what is not given*, at a *distant goal*, points to connection and continuity so that 'the division between the being relation and ought relation is in a certain way analogous to that between sensation and representation' (separation and conjunction).[31] Accordingly, in the ought relation, the fixated positing of the being relation dissolves into the continuity, the manifold of the discrete into the unity of the continuous. Furthermore, that means that sensation and representation are to be posited not only as potency of the positing of being, of the theoretical, but also of the ought relation, that is that they must also take up the moment of striving into their concept. In sensation there is 'drive', in representation 'aspiration' and in thinking 'direction'.

With this a schema is attained that no content of consciousness can elude, which, according to the type of its composition, points to an infinite progression and justifies this development as necessary. It therefore suggests itself to also ask about an upper limit of consciousness. That limit is again only ideational, but firmly determined as guiding point: the pure determinedness, actuality, the antipode of pure potency, the pure consciousness of consciousness in which the polarity of consciousness and object is superseded (νόησις νοήσεως).

In this way, *the whole of the inventory of consciousness* is, in terms of its *kind*, marked off, but it remains at the level of general schemas. All specification only gets to ever lower kinds, but the concrete itself, that which is properly psychical, is not yet attained with that. It remains at the level of 'subjective bases in general for objectifications in general'.[32] One does not yet see how there is in these fundamental categories a sufficient basis for a method that approximates what, in concrete living experience, is ultimately immediate in its integrity.

What has been achieved until now is only a general description of the kinds of consciousness (phenomenology), a first, 'however powerful and central province of psychology'.[33] The general possibilities 'of what can be experienced at all'[34] are pre-delineated in this way: the pure, the lawful, the a priori, the 'eidos', in the relating back to which everything 'impure is conceptualized to the extent to which it is at all capable of this'.[35] (Preconception of something 'pure' formulated in a particular way

DESTRUCTING CONSIDERATION OF THE NATORPIAN POSITION

(constitution!), characterizing and determining the limits of subjectification itself. 'Conceptualize' in which sense? Concept!)

But how does one get from the pure possibilities to the actuality of living experience itself in its *concretion*? What seems to matter essentially here is the relating of the content of lived experience back to the experiencing *I*. However, 'we do not have in advance an experiencing 'I' but we first have to constitute such an 'I', namely in the greatest possible range of this expression of the problem, according to its psychological concept'.[36] (In which situation and problem situation!)

Natorp characterizes it as a 'decisive step towards the clarification of the matter' that one becomes aware of the fact that only – after, on the basis of a general phenomenology, clarity is attained about the possible content of consciousness – the question about the 'I' in general can be posed in a methodologically justifiable way.

With this question a second major task of psychology is posed, that regarding the *distinction of the unities of lived experience*.[37] Psychology does not ask about the abstract unity of consciousness but about the concrete unities. It therefore first has to ask about the *distinction as arising out of which this plurality of unities of lived experience is to be thought*. This distinction enacts itself in analogous sequence like the task of phenomenology. This task, too, as a psychological one, finds itself referred to objectifications. Since phenomenology goes on ahead with its fundamental divisions, one can now easily locate the unities of lived experience corresponding to the levels of consciousness and directions of consciousness because every kind of objectification corresponds to a subject, an *I or something constituting*.

'The stage of sensation obviously corresponds to the absolutely individual *moment* of lived experience; the concrete, always specifically delimited conjunction in the representation corresponds to the concrete, specifically delimited *complex* of lived experience which demarcates itself in the unity of living experience, which is each time relative, from the each time experiencing "I"; the comprehensive, ideational unity of conceptual thought corresponds to the comprehensive ideational *unity* of consciousness, the pure "I".'[38] These levels of unity are now organized among themselves like potency and act. The 'I' of the lived experience of the moment e.g. is only potency with regard to the 'I' of the delimited complex of lived experience in representation. But this 'I' which already possesses an act character appears once again in the potencies 'with regard to the more strict actualization which is only attained in the comprehensive consciousness of thinking'.[39] In the highest unity, it turns out that the 'I' is no longer an individual 'I' at all but already a universal consciousness, an ideal subject 'in general'.

'As something distinctive the 'I' therefore basically exists only on the level of representation, and exactly for this reason never in full actuality.'[40] This transfers itself 'accordingly' from the being relation to the ought relation and the analogous levels with respect to the 'I' of the will [*Willens-Ich*].

'Limit categories': 'In the sense of such methodological positing of limits, by the way, the already touched-upon lower limit will also correspond to an upper one in the 'I'-relationship as well as in the relationship of content. If now one of them [...] is posited on this side of all delimited [...] unity of lived experience, [...] then the other one is posited beyond any delimitation.'[41, 42] The discretion and continuity of the unity of lived experience goes genuinely and consistently together with that of the content.[43] These ideal limit categories are indispensable; within them, forwards and backwards, every positive consciousness is determined, to which often still belongs the consciousness of this distance from the limits (e.g. religious consciousness).[44]

§ 14. The carrying-out of the destruction

(a) In which tendency does Natorp approach the complex of lived experience?

The viewpoints or the questions that guide the destruction do not form a schema but are taken so formally that they do not prejudge anything, it is rather that the peculiar character of the position in question becomes apparent in the manner in which they concretely merge in the pursuit in various sense-complexes, that is, in the manner of the complex.

The peculiar character of Natorp's position is precisely that the four questions finally converge *in one*, which in itself – disregarding the formal separation, not in terms of attitude – is in no way the case, as it will turn out.

The tendency towards the apprehension of the complex of lived experience is characterized by two moments that could formally meet unquestionable approval: 1. The complex of lived experience is seen; in mind is a goal as full concretion, as the absolute vitality, as process, as actuality, as immediate character of the soul. 2. A relation of apprehension is sought in which this totality is to be had in the greatest possible approximation

DESTRUCTING CONSIDERATION OF THE NATORPIAN POSITION

and strictness, at least as far as it is possible according to its sense (to conceptualize it).

(Precedence of the method from which unity and manifoldness determine themselves, with which they are determined. (a) The problem of lived experience, essentially motivated by the question of method, initiated by the method itself. (b) Therefore the question of method is itself primary with respect to the initiated problem of lived experience. Provided that the problem of method is a problem in the correlation to objectivity, the correlation itself must also be incorporated in the ultimate problematic.)

The method of reconstruction is attained as a relation of apprehension in which the tendency fulfils itself. Method means way, direction, strictly lawfully guided step-complex of instances of attaining knowledge. The complex of lived experience is determined in its totality according to this method, its primacy before any fixed content of subject matter. As certainly as the limits are never reached in the infinity of the task of attaining knowledge, as clearly and specifically are they themselves *fixed by* the method as the infinitely distant points towards which the movement of the method according to its own sense strives.

This primacy of the method that is characteristic for the philosophy of the Marburg school and its understanding of knowledge must be kept in view in order to purely understand the starting point of the problem of lived experience. The relation of apprehension is in itself firmly predetermined and with it *its* task; it provides the structure and limits of the domain that is to be apprehended. The question about the manner of the possible having of lived experiences precedes every other question containing subject matter. Only from there and *within* the method is the fundamental constitution of what is to be apprehended determined.

A method is most securely determined in connection with a comprehensive method, to be precise, as a specification of the latter or else in opposition to it. The first given method of attaining knowledge is the determination of objects. The latter shows the curious fact that with it and through it a whole lot is set aside, not fortuitously but necessarily required by its tendencies. As something that is set aside by the objectifying knowledge – required by the sense – it can therefore never actually objectifyingly be apprehended but only in the opposite direction of knowledge, i.e. only subjectifyingly. From the method as such and its task a remainder arises which as remainder *of this method requires* another method for its apprehension ('requires' – on the basis of which preconception? constitution). The opposite side, the addition, is an addition to this specific method and has to supersede *the latter's* limit. The sense of the supersession is therefore pre-delineated by the sense of the *lack* that is to be superseded. We only have to radically think to the end the being-dependent of the new (here of the subjectifying) method on a pre-given one and construct it from there. At the same time the requirement arises from the primacy of the *method* to fix and firmly determine its entire structural complex beforehand – before any concrete apprehension of objects. The a priori fundamental relationships and fundamental categories are not only presupposed in terms of subject matter and in themselves (τῇ φύσει), they do not only – transcendentally speaking – 'underlie', but are, according to the primacy of the method, to be elaborated as the latter's structural components even before a concrete putting-to-work of the method. Only on the basis, therefore, of the thoroughgoing methodological predetermination and constitution of the domain is an adequate and strict concrete investigation of it possible at all and the fumbling, the directionless beginning and the fragmenting description are brought to an end.

The question, therefore, of how lived experiences are had is taken from the beginning as that of the method of attaining knowledge and as question of method is therefore inserted into the general problematic of method so that the theoretical relation of apprehension is essentially determined from a comprehensive and essentially counter-directed one. Especially with respect to the having of the complex of lived experience, the question of method is the first and the last because after all here it is about the apprehension of the full concretion, about that of the individual in its immediacy. 'In this way the ultimate individual remains undetermined of course if "determine" is supposed to mean to determine completely, work *out*; remains unknown if "knowing" is supposed to mean being *totally* versed in. However, all the more is *de*termined, *re*cognized in it if one thinks of the function, the way and the nowhere inhibited progression, not of an absolute goal which is to be reached.'[1]

Only from the primacy of the method, more specifically from the latter's predetermining lawfulness, arises the fundamental constitution of the domain, of the complex of lived experience and also arises the *methodological* hierarchy and order according to subject matter, the sense-complex of the problems.

[Comment concerning the 1. destructing question:]

(a) the problem of lived experience is motivated essentially by the question of *method, initiated* by the *method* itself, namely as a result of the specific sense of lived experience as something subjective; b) therefore the question of method is itself primary with respect to the initiated problem of lived experience.

(b) Which is the character of unity and manifoldness of the complex of lived experience?

Provided that the method is all determining, that which we are aiming at in the second question is determined from the method itself. And provided that psychology is concerned with the full ultimate concretion, the fundamental constitution of this concrete will only come forward in such a way that the problem of method itself is radically grasped. Along with what is most primordial in the method, simultaneously the basic structure of the concrete is firmly determined. It was already shown how the subjectification is always and strictly correlative of the objectification. It is therefore absolutely necessary to apprehend this correlativity in its ultimate grounds. That would be a deeper psychology that 'seeks to grasp both, the objective and the subjective, as much as possible, in its ultimate depth'.[2]

It is the danger of transcendental philosophy that one 'unquestionably accepts' subjectivity ('I' is not equivalent to subjectivity) 'and then seeks to conjure up objectivity from it';[3] to objectify and reify subjectivity itself, i.e. to see it in the fixed constitution – instead of in the movement! The question of the relationship between objectivity and subjectivity must therefore be posed in the most comprehensive scope that encompasses all directions of objectification (knowledge). This question about the relation between objectivity and subjectivity can only be securely and purely decided in connection with the question of general logic – 'a logic of synthetic, not merely (like the "general" logic of Kant) analytical thinking'.[4] 'No other standpoint is radical enough for this purpose.'[5] This question is *the* question of method.

Let us take account strictly of how our two viewpoints of destruction relate to one another. From the first viewpoint we pose the 'more abstract' question, namely what the tendency of having and the aspect of what is to be apprehended looks like in general. From the second viewpoint, we then pose the more concrete question as to which are the specific characters of unity and manifoldness. This more concrete question leads into the carrying-out of the Natorpian position, in fact this is based in its fundamental particularity on *even* more general questions, on the ultimate system questions of philosophy in general.

Then, however, it must at the same time also become apparent here how in this ultimate system ground the two problem groups – problem of the a priori and problem of lived experience – unite.

The question is about the character of unity and manifoldness of the complex of lived experience in its full concretion. 'Potency' is regarded as the fundamental category, and it was characterized as the properly 'system-forming concept'. With this the question about the unity of the manifold of the complex of lived experience could be settled. But it only begins in the strict formulation of the concept of potency itself. It is the question about what is systematically encompassed in it and how – structurally – this unity of the manifold is to be grasped.

The idea of potency leads – thought out to the end – to pure potency or to the immediate that is not yet articulated through any division and differentiation, which lies *before* the articulation, i.e. at the same time before actuality. It therefore leads to a lower limit but equally to an upper limit in which all potentiality disappears into pure actuality, into pure determining and being-determined. Ultimately, even if conceptually always separated, the two limits coincide. Between them lie the non-pure potentiality and the non-pure actuality. This between is what can actually be experienced and contains the basic divisions into levels of consciousness and directions of consciousness. *Their* unification results in the ultimate concretion. We know: the unification can only be one of ultimate primordial methodology in which also the correlation of objectification and subjectification *may* no longer be emphasized unilaterally in the direction of objectification or that of subjectification. (From where is this 'may' dictated?)

As far as the two basic divisions in their relation to one another are at first concerned, it has to be said that actually the direction, that of the ought, underlies the levels and that according to subject matter the division into levels is integrated in the division into directions. Thinking itself, the highest level in which the other two (separation and conjunction) merge into pure correlation, is itself to be thought as 'act', 'striving' in the ought relation[6] so that the problem of the ultimate concretion of the complex of lived experience, of its unity, intensifies towards the question about the concrete unification of ought and being (existence), a problem that 'is strived for in Kant's system but is not reached'.[7] It is the question 'about the system-ground of the distinction between the theoretical and the practical in general and about the exact sense of their final unity in "one and the same reason"'.[8] In Kant, lines for the solution of this system question are pre-delineated but it is still necessary to independently think Kant to the end here.

'Already since Fichte it is by far insufficient to repeat that theoretical and practical reason are one insofar as here and there we are dealing with 'validity' – logical validity of knowledge there, validity of will here.'[9] Neither is it sufficient to say that finally the theory of knowledge 'is eventually itself based on an ought in the objective sense',[10] namely as the primacy of the practical reason of the ought also in logic and philosophy in general. Natorp says: 'Theory is not as such purpose-directed, knowledge is not as such [according to its sense] a matter of will, although one certainly seeks knowledge'.[11] Kant did not examine knowledge as something that 'ought to be'. It could rather be said that he based the ought on judgment, knowledge. 'Knowledge always remains for him the generic concept.'[12] 'Will is also knowledge.'[13]

The problem at hand, which is not brought up and engaged, is to be posed in this way: 'Which are the ultimate principles or categorial bases that are equally valid for both domains, and then how from the common ultimate and in fact logical ground the first division that is fundamental for all further divisions flows with logical necessity into the two directions of the theoretical and practical'.[14] The problem of an ultimate general (primal) logic arises and not of an analytically formal one (in Kant's sense), the logic of the object, the determination of the object as such, from which all special directions of knowing, of the positing of the object (of all objectification and subjectification) 'must first arise from as necessary radiations'.[15] Without this 'inevitable generalization of the transcendental problem [...] the system-thought can however, on transcendental grounds, not be ultimately clarified'.[16]

In this way, the two fundamental problems are indicated, the posing and solving of which the further development of the philosophical system quite simply depends on: 1. The question about 'the *ultimate generalization* of the problem of the logical'.[17] 2. The question of 'its *ultimate intensification* towards the question of the *individual*',[18] of the ultimate concretion, of the full concretion. With regard to this, Natorp remarks that contemporary philosophy finds itself, from the most differing motives, directed towards these ultimate system questions and that from this fact the solely valid instruction as to direction becomes understandable. According to him, the more farseeing among the younger generation also are no longer interested in scholastic isolation and the insistence on school traditions.

How is this logic of the origin to be thought now, this ultimate that also still underlies the opposition between objectivity and subjectivity and only from which the basic structures (unity and manifoldness) of both are ultimately known? In order to apprehend this we proceed from the ultimate intensification of the logical, namely from the individual. About this it must be said that it, 'as that which is intentionally determined, not only in general requires logical determination but rather the highest and ultimate logical determination'.[19] The singularity of the individual is determinable only 'synthetically in a literally "infinitely" consolidated sense'.[20]

The problem of the individual presents itself as that of specification within a commonality. But it is determined not as the instance of the genus but through the law of the sequence. Through this law the individual is fully determined, it is there through it and in it, exists. But also in this way it still remains undetermined, still abstract, because it is determined each time only with regard to *one* of its moments in its sequential lawfulness. In its existence [*Dasein*], in its existence [*Existenz*] the individual is only determined through the order of existence itself, i.e. in the 'infinite-fold, infinitely dimensional infinite and for exactly that reason fully determined continuum *of* existence [*Dasein*]'.[21] The ultimate individual and concrete is never completely determined, never 'worked out'. But all the more is determined and known in it when it is not formulated as a finite fixed point, as a fixed goal, but when the *function*, the *way* and the progression is thought of.

The concrete is not the a-logical, not logically amorphous. It is only not logically fully determined if I look at it abstractly, in just any respect. Natorp: 'I assert in contrast the full logicality, the full formedness, the thoroughly being-formed of the purportedly a-logical.'[22] It is not outside the logical, outside the lawful. In its full pure lawfulness, it can only be apprehended in going back, in reflection. Objectively, abstractly it is only unilaterally determined. 'It *itself* however knows *itself* to be quite simply determined, that is, quite simply formed [...] That means: it *is*.'[23] (As long as it is merely determined in the objectification, it is always determined only abstractly, *unilaterally*; in reflection it knows itself to be in the all-ness of the infinite relationships of determination.)

'With this: "It itself knows itself" to be like that, it is however already pointed to the ultimate which this train of thought inevitably presses towards: A "self' and an 'itself" is only there for a *knowing*, which as such is necessarily at the same time knowing *itself*.'[24] The full being-its-own

DESTRUCTING CONSIDERATION OF THE NATORPIAN POSITION

does not yet reach the mathematically, physically, biologically or as 'person' practically determined; but only *that which* knows *itself* to be in the counter-relation to the absolute *universitas*, to God, is fully determined. 'For this reason "God", for the self that knows itself, is not merely a matter of "belief" in whatever sense that holds open a possible sensible doubt, but it *knows* "God" as surely as, and entirely in the same sense in which it knows itself.'[25] Leibniz and Plato probably already more than suspected this. In this correlation in the system not only knowledge becomes possible but movement, power, the soul, God. 'The ultimate concrete is only given in *consciousness* knowing itself, with regard to which all mere objectivity remains an abstraction.'[26]

'Only the thinking of the origin itself can discover itself, precisely in that it becomes aware of the entire content of consciousness as generated from the origin.'[27] That is the ultimate justification from the origin, the ultimate logical. The full concretion lies in the absolute self-consciousness of the thinking of the origin and positing.

That is by no means some psychological idealism. Considered from the side of the subject, subjectivity appears as the basis of objectivity, provided that the latter constitutes itself in subjectivity. 'But considered logically', subjectivity is rather to be explained as the opposite side of objectification, of determination, of consciousness, because the latter is determination, positing in unity. This relational unity and primal unity is the primal lived experience. It is therefore neither subjective nor objective idealism, but idealism of the origin or absolute idealism if one attaches importance to terms.

The genuine 'energy' (actuality, vitality, concretion), the genuine life of the psyche can only lie in the supra-temporal complex (of primal thinking, of primal logic).[28] From this ultimate system ground of the unity of the positing and determination, the unity of subjectivity, of the complex of lived experience, is determined. Being-its-own, full and ultimate concretion only happens in the primal positing of the thinking of the origin and of its infinite progress in the correlativity of the determinations (objective and subjective ones). In this primal thinking the 'I', the pure 'I' is merely the ultimate point of reference of the relationship that as such is determination, conjunction and therefore concretion, concretion in the infinite process. In the ultimate concrete there is therefore no 'I' in the sense of a concrete and delimitable separate-'I' to be found.

THE CARRYING-OUT OF THE DESTRUCTION

(c) How does the 'I' comport itself in the complex of lived experience?

Wherever such a separate 'I' is asked about – as the question about the concrete unities of lived experience in the carrying-out of psychology – it turns out that such concrete separate 'I's are themselves only constituted through the whole of the complex of lived experience, which ultimately is rooted in the already indicated primal ground. (In this way also the concrete question about the position of the 'I' within the complex of lived experience is dissolved as a stage in the process of the method.)

The question of how the concrete 'I' comports itself in the complex of lived experience is each time a special question in terms of content with respect to consciousness, namely the question about the unitary character of a manifoldness of something conscious, because other than in the conscious content the 'I' is not given and also cannot be given. The specific unity-complex itself may not become isolated and immobilized but, as this concrete form of unity of consciousness, is always to be traced back to the ultimate concrete in which it is grasped as an origin.

The 'I' is therefore not a problem of psychology, it is not a problem at all but the ultimate problem ground of every problematic. Because in anything that is asked, in all that is conscious, the 'I' is already presupposed. So that in general our third question is not misunderstood and too much is asked in it, the question is to be decided how and whether at all the 'I' is a possible object of consciousness. This question again leads back to the first one. From that it already becomes evident that for Natorp in principle any concrete problem of the 'I' is in some sense secondary and derivative.

(d) How is the 'I' itself had?

The 'I' as such is not at all a possible object of consciousness. It is, therefore, not conceptually graspable, i.e. we are not in the position 'to coordinate it with something else, as something which is logically equal, and to subordinate it to a third, as something which is logically higher'.[29] It is no possible content of a consciousness but exactly that which is conscious of something.

'Being 'I' means not to be object, but to be, with regard to every object, that for which alone something is object.'[30] Although it cannot be forbidden to speak about the 'I', that is to objectify it – in fact it even must be done – but it must be just as clear that then it is no longer itself. If it were itself grasped and graspable as the 'I', then it would be 'at the same time something knowing and something known, at the same time subject and object of one and the same act of knowing'.[31] But that 'contradicts the appearance. An act like representation, knowledge, consciousness in general cannot possibly be thought in such a way that subject and object of this act would be, in terms of content and numerically, the same in every respect'.[32] It would have to, though, if the 'I' as such should be able to be an object of thinking. The 'I' is already no longer thought as 'I' when it is thought as an object. 'But in thinking alone one becomes conscious of the 'I' as such.'[33]

Predicates such as existence [*Dasein*], factuality, existence [*Existenz*] cannot be attributed to the 'I' in the same sense as these propositions are usually understood. For every proposition – also that of existence – the 'I' (consciousness) is already a presupposition. Therefore the 'I' cannot be subordinated to the concept of existence. The 'I' is merely a point of reference for everything that is conscious, it is ground of all facts and of all being given and therefore is not itself given. Just as little as the 'I' as the ultimate point of reference can be described, is the relationship of the 'I' to the conscious something, the consciousness [*die Bewußtheit*], describable. The latter is something irreducibly ultimate. All so-called descriptions are descriptions of the conscious as such, of the content of consciousness. Consciousness is relationship and 'relating means: to keep apart and at the same time unite in a consciousness, to be precise, in *one* consciousness'.[34] Unification and separation, unity of the manifoldnesses can only be apprehended in the content of consciousness, not as actions. Also concrete empirical separate 'I's are not separated objects but can be encountered as each time different forms of unity of the respective manifoldness of the content of consciousness. In every description of the 'I', one borrows from the content that is precisely conscious content for the 'I' and to which therefore the idea of unity, the relationship to the 'I' unity forms the basis. This relationship to the 'I' does not in turn present itself, this 'opposite' itself is not in turn object.

The question can only be how a manifoldness of the content of consciousness, which happens to be at hand, fits into (includes itself in) a concrete unity and into which one. That immediately points to how this relative unity relates to the absolute and primordial unity of the pure relationship and determination of primal thinking. The problem is 'the particular way in which each time (namely for each psychological deliberation, from each viewpoint of any such deliberation) the content of consciousness presents itself in unity. [...] The relative unity itself however belongs to the content because the "form", i.e. the kind of unification, belongs no less than the "matter", the elements which are to be united, to the content, literally to the interior content of consciousness, is indeed what essentially constitutes the latter. For content means: a manifold in unity, matter in form'.[35] Provided that each concrete 'I' unity is such a unity as constituted, in this and that way constituted complex of lived experience, in fact according to its content [*Inhalt*] (content accordingly [*gehaltsmäßig*]), the talk about particular manners of consciousness, of the relationship of the 'I' to the content and different 'I's subsisting next to the content is not only superfluous but also psychologically not verifiable. Natorp's position with regard to this question is well suited to illuminate more sharply what he understands by content of consciousness, 'existence' in consciousness.

One believes to find in every 'modification of consciousness', in sensation, representation, thinking, feeling, desiring, willing – 'apart from the consciousness of the sensed, represented, thought, felt, desired, wanted still a consciousness of sensation, representation, thinking, feeling, desiring, willing as of our doing' 'and that therein the conscious-ness and the conscious 'I' receives its concrete determination'.[36]

Certainly two things are to be distinguished through abstraction: the existence of the content and its relation to the 'I'. The latter, however, cannot be considered in a separate way, but 'the indescribable opposite to the 'I' is always already implied in the existence of the content for the one who each time senses, represents, etc.'[37] Existence of a content is belongingness to 'me', i.e. the content is 'component' of my present consciousness; it integrates into the concrete unity of lived experience. Existence is this integrating into. (Transcendental interpretation of the subject clear here!) If I leave out the content, e.g. the heard sound, nothing remains for me; with it also disappears the consciousness and the 'I'.

Only ways of insertions can be pointed out. And Natorp now seeks to confirm the thesis in detail for the sensible elementary contents, for content conjunctions, for feeling and striving.

In the case of the ultimate elementary units of consciousness – the pure contents of sensation – it would, provided that they are indeed mere matter, strictly speaking be inappropriate to talk at all about form or unity of the conjunction. Individual sensations and the classes of sensations are sufficiently differentiated by their content; one will not want to characterize the being-conscious [*Bewußthaben*] of a sound as opposed to a colour as differing in terms of kind. 'Certainly we do in fact "feel" different when we hear and when we see; but this difference apparently no longer concerns the pure content of sensation but depends on various accompanying moments that are partly difficult to grasp, on complexes be it on the basis of sensations of different classes or such with moments of feeling and striving.'[38]

The same arises in the case of the representations (content conjunctions); the conjunction and lack of conjunction (spatial and temporal) is always to be pointed out in the content, 'in the content, precisely in the way we are conscious of it, and not in addition in the being-conscious [*Bewußtsein*] of the content',[39] in a manner of consciousness.

Feeling and striving though rather seem to point to a peculiar comportment of the 'I' so that here it may be difficult to disregard a particular manner of consciousness and of the 'I' itself. Natorp concedes that moments of feeling and striving cannot be put together from pure sensations, that they are more than 'external' complexes of that kind, that in them, however close their relationship to representation may be in any case, 'there still prevails in any case an inner relation among the elements of representation which one may describe as "tending" in terms of its most general character, a relation that perhaps is rooted deeper than anything else in primal lived experience'.[40] But in spite of this these difficult to grasp moments as well are 'included as something conscious to me, experienced by me, in the "content" of consciousness [...]'.[41] If one takes into account this broad sense of content of consciousness, then it becomes evident how also here consciousness is not something separated but coincides with the existence of the content of consciousness as a whole, its respective unity. Also the moments of feeling and striving are experienced as much as the mere content of representation, simply as moments of content in consciousness; striving and feeling as well can be content of consciousness. And provided that the fundamental character of the consciousness is conjunction – relationship, separation and unification – the moment of tendency also lies therein, 'as it were, as attraction and repulsion'.[42] To appear 'in' consciousness means: being apperceived.

'Consciousness as a manifoldness is to be regarded not merely from one or some, but probably from infinite dimensions.'[43] There is no *isolation* in consciousness. There is separation, but always only as a kind of relationship and conjunction, precisely in *one* consciousness. Consciousness *consists*, in terms of its content, *in conjunction*. 'Content' simply means: subsistence. This subsistence is a lawful one, to be precise, the ultimate lawfulness, the *primal law* of the *universitas* (God) of the conjunctions.

At this point, the consistent thinking through and thinking to the end of the problem of the 'I' in Natorp's psychology as a whole has led us back to the point of departure. In other words, the individual, provided that it knows itself in opposition to this *universitas* as the latter's opposing direction, is itself in this way determined in the primal lawfulness and the problem of the a priori (law in the objectifying direction) in its relationship to the subject is dissolved and superseded – in the primal logic.

It is now necessary to sharply bring out the guiding preconception; to sharply, i.e. in the manner in which it determines and intersperses the entire problematic, make this guiding preconception visible so as to have it, as purely brought out, thus available for dijudication.

§ 15 Constitution as guiding preconception

(a) The primacy of the method

Pursuing the four questions resulted in a constant pointing back to the question of method. Also the problem of the 'I' is determined from this primacy. The 'I' is not at all an object of possible questioning, not a problem, but a problem ground, the presupposition of all questioning.

Every concrete separate 'I' is, as a concrete one, the unity of a manifoldness, that is, a particular conscious thing [*Bewußtes*], belonging in the content of consciousness. Therefore the concrete problem of the 'I' becomes part of the general question of method of determining the unity of consciousness. The problem of the 'I' therefore – as a concrete one – methodologically already presupposes general questions about the unity of consciousness, its levels and directions. It does not stand there as a closed circle of problems with a specifically required methodology. The methodological question of unity regarding consciousness presses towards the radical ultimate grounding of ultimate opposites and ultimate manifoldness in an ultimate primordial unity. Objectivity and subjectivity are not separated, neither of them outweighs the other, they consist *in* correlation, in relationship. Relationship and self-determining in relationship complexes, to be precise, infinite self-determining in the progression of knowledge, on the way of knowledge, in the method of thinking is the most primordial.

From this primacy of the method the construction of psychology, the sequence of the problems, is determined not only in its logical connections but with regard to the factual order of the possible concrete carrying-out and completion.

Why primacy of the method? Is it merely asserted and blindly posited? Or does the sense-complex of this entire position in itself and in its most tangible exponent – that is, the primacy of the method – point towards an underlying motive? If we maintain a concrete position in the entire sense-complex and move within the way it points forward and backward and pose the question of understanding about the primordial motive, then it becomes apparent how it is grounded in a specific preconception: *in the positing of the idea of constitution as the radical and universal guiding idea.* For not only is that which is conscious, the *objectified* posited as constituted but – since it is after all about the subjective, the psychical – also the latter, to be precise, in a radicalized idea of constitution, in a reckless thinking to the end of the thought of constitution, which alone makes it understandable that this idea is capable of encompassing the entire problematic of philosophy and giving it the completeness with which it presents itself in the entire system. Constitution means to say: *constitution in consciousness.* Consciousness is, however, not understood as a special domain of subject matter, as an arsenal of categories, but in its pure formulation as unity of the determination of a manifold of relationships. Consciousness as relationship; relationship: reference of one to the other, of the other to the one, that is progression, to be precise, progression in ultimate lawfulness.

From this preconception, the sense of the complex of lived experience, of concretion, immediacy, vitality, actuality, individuality and subjectivity, the sense of 'I', that of the 'I' unity as well as that of the concrete 'I' is determined. *From this preconception,* the kind of the actually possible direction of questioning about the relation of the apprehension of the complex of lived experience on the whole as a task and about that relation in the specification of the actually possible apprehension of the 'I' is determined.

In the idea of constitution the sense of ultimate a priori lawfulness (norm) is determined unitarily just as that of the individual and the concrete. It is here, therefore, that the problem of the a priori is resolved in a strictly unitary way. The rigid opposition and separateness of the a priori and individual singular occurring is superseded and therefore the question of the μέθεζις and participation.

From there arises the unity of the interpretation of Plato that is not historical in the sense that it does not remain within the means of interpretation that were available to Plato himself; by way of contrast, it nevertheless properly understands Plato in the sense that it radically thinks him to the end. (Therefore, for example, also Spengler's morphological *construction* of ancient and Christian thinking is something provisional that remains on the outside and makes a philosophy of history out of the externality.)

It shall now be briefly pursued how this preconception determines the problem of lived experience, its form and its concrete individual questions in order to then understand by means of contrast as sharply as possible how this preconception veers away from the direction that is predelineated by the motive of philosophizing, so that with it something is answered and asked that philosophy does not want to enquire into because it does not at all enquire in the theoretical sense but cares after [*nachsorgt*]. (Destruction: to intensify the concern [*Sorge*] and to concentrate it on existence; dijudication: initiate fundamental experience, *decision-concern*, 'desperation'.)

The consistent determination of the problem of lived experience through the preconception of constitution must most coarsely leap into view in concrete contexts. We shall therefore first discuss the problem of the 'I'.

(b) The determination of the problem of the 'I' through the idea of constitution

When primordially and decisively characterizing the 'I', when determining its sense, Natorp strives to prejudge as little as possible or not at all. According to him, not even existence [*Dasein*], factuality or existence [*Existenz*] are predicated to it, no concrete determination containing subject matter; indeed, it is not supposed to be made into a problem at all, it is merely the *problem ground* of psychology and therefore of philosophy in general. It is no possible object of consciousness at all but that for which everything objective is object.

And yet this empty positing that prejudges nothing, of the 'I' as point of reference is only apparently without presupposition and apparently 'primordial'. It is primordial only in terms of a specific idea, a preconception with respect to which the question arises whether it is

DESTRUCTING CONSIDERATION OF THE NATORPIAN POSITION

primordial in the sense of the motivation of all philosophy. 'I' is problem ground only for a problematic that is pervaded by the idea of constitution. The positing therefore has its sense only in the idea of constitution. 'I' as problem ground, as ground of all givenness, is the 'I think' that must be able to accompany all consciousness. Thus the 'I' is assigned a very specific role, to be precise, the decisive and primordial one, namely to be the ground of all constitution, the unity of everything manifold in consciousness.

Still disregarding *how* it is argued, in order to demonstrate the impossibility of its being-an-object according to its own sense, already the fact *that* an attempt is made in this direction to predicate something on the 'I' or rather to keep all predication [*Aussage*] away from it, shows that it is determined from the idea of constitution.

One has already ceased to think the 'I' as 'I' if one 'thinks' it as object. If it were itself had as 'I' then it would be at the same time something knowing and something known. That is impossible because it underlies thinking and knowing, is presupposed by them. And exactly that which is presupposed by thinking and knowing is the 'I'. Precisely because it cannot function as object of thinking it is thought as related to thinking, as underlying thinking. Its unthinkability places its sense as related to thinking, as *theoretical* thinking 'I' and knowledge 'I' into the brightest light. It is determined exactly from thinking, to be precise, from the thinking to the end of thinking. This sense of *I-ness* is the primordial and remains the constantly dominating one.

Natorp does not at all pose the question whether the 'I' is, in fact, supposed to be *thought*, whether its sense must necessarily and can solely determine itself in thinking – as correlate of thinking. From the fact that the argumentation with respect to the possibility of the objectification of the 'I' as 'I' is placed at the forefront as decisive it only follows that from the beginning onwards the problem of the 'I' is pressed into a quite specific direction: that the 'I' has the role of the ultimate presupposition of unity of consciousness as the constituting one and that from this sense of unity of thinking every concrete question of unity, i.e. every question of consciousness and of lived experience is determined.

All relationship to this point of reference, to this 'I', i.e. the consciousness, is something ultimate that is not further determinable. Everything has this simple relationship that consists in the fact that the 'I' is point of unity of something manifold – unification. That is only the same sense of the 'I' that is determined from the idea of constitution, with regard to what it is conscious of. Natorp, as it were, inverts what is meant by intentionality, the relationship of the 'I' to what is conscious, the consciousness becomes the relationship to the point of reference.

If this sense of 'I'-ness is steadily and everywhere maintained, i.e. if one in no way strays in this particular sense-giving from the idea of constitution, if one seeks to determine consciousness in the light of this idea and with this concept of the 'I' as fundamental, then a determination can a priori only relate to what is conscious, the content of consciousness. 'I' and consciousness are an ultimate; each concrete separate 'I' is constituted, i.e. pointing back towards the proper and ultimate 'I'. Likewise, everything that is addressed as different manners and kinds of consciousness (intentionality) is diversity of the constitution, of the unity of the manifold of the content of consciousness. The discourse about acts and activities is the sign of a reification of consciousness, i.e. of a non-considering of the latter from the constant viewpoint of *constitution*!

Being-conscious, existing in consciousness, being content means once again *being constituted*, being the unity of a manifold. Consciousness, existing in consciousness, is comprehended from the sense of the constituting 'I'. 'I hear the sound', 'I see the colour' means 'the sound is there', 'the colour is there' in consciousness, as component of a complex of lived experience, fitting into it. Consciousness, existence for an 'I', consciousness means precisely being constituted. And all content of consciousness is constituted. The sense of this existence is the same everywhere. Hearing and seeing are not different manners of consciousness but only *what* is there, *what* is constituted, is different; and its connectedness of content and form of unity is different, but the being unified has the same sense everywhere – consciousness.

Natorp nevertheless concedes that for us hearing feels different than seeing, but he says this depended on various accompanying moments that are in part difficult to grasp – complexes of sensation, feeling and striving moments.[1] The question, however, is not what that depends on but whether it is not exactly understandable only from hearing as hearing and seeing as seeing, to what extent we feel in one way when we see and in another way when we hear. (Natorp takes 'feeling' merely as something happening, something that is simply there in consciousness.) If I focus on the 'pure content of sensation', however, i.e. if I switch off the feeling while hearing and seeing and take into view the pure sound data and pure colour data and then ask in what way I am conscious of these data, then indeed something different comes to light. This being conscious is the same with sound and colour and every sensation datum. But then I neither have any longer what I see and hear and also no longer the being-conscious of hearing, if one may at all say so; because I can neither 'see' nor 'hear' a sensation datum, just as little as I can see or hear the *being-constituted* about which Natorp rightly asserts that he could not emulate anyone in it.

Here the reinterpreting and sense-determining influence of the preconception of the idea of constitution – one would almost like to say – can be grasped with hands. Hearing and seeing is understood as the being-constituted of a colour datum respectively sound datum in the unity of a consciousness. *Already a priori and according to its sense, the question that is guided by the preconception forbids seeing a distinction at all.*

In the same way representations are from the beginning comprehended and defined, under the guiding presupposition and as a consequence of it, as nothing else than conjunctions of content. Since representing again just as sensing means: existing in consciousness, being constituted, the distinction is settled as one of different unities of the conjunction of contents.

Still stronger is the reinterpretation of the lived experiences of feeling and striving (disregarding the coarse exemplification in general). Also these moments, which are difficult to grasp, are 'as something that I am conscious of', as experienced by me included in the content of consciousness. I.e., provided that they are there, fit into a complex, constitute themselves – however much they may still be something 'deeper', what remains decisive: they are contents of consciousness and they happen, they fit in; in the manner of fitting in I have *consciousness*.

The concrete 'I's are as concretions of the 'abstract' only certain forms of unity of manifoldnesses of the respective contents of consciousness, complexes of lived experience.

Consequently, it may now have become clear how radically and consistently the entire problem of the 'I' is determined by the idea of constitution as a concrete problem as well as in its ultimate primordiality where the 'I' can only still be posited as problem *ground*. It is, therefore, not only the case that what is objective constitutes itself in consciousness, but what is there in consciousness – the conscious as such and in every respect – constitutes itself and subjectivity. Reconstruction is nothing other than the apprehension of the constitution complex in the subjective direction. The subjective is that which regressively constitutes itself, namely the constituting [?] forming of unity of what is set aside in the objectification.

CONSTITUTION AS GUIDING PRECONCEPTION

The system-forming concept of psychology – the 'potency' or condition of possibility – is a specifically constitutional concept. The discourse about an upper and lower limit of consciousness is only comprehensible from the viewpoint of the idea of constitution. Concretion means to say nothing other than all-round completed constitution complex, the entirety of the constitutive relationships in the unity and correlativity of consciousness. Consciousness is unifying and separating in the unity of consciousness. Consciousness is therefore relationship, while the relationship logically precedes the points of reference. Relationship is the ultimate, and the infinite relationship complex of objectification and subjectification in their correlativity constitutes the concrete. ('Enactment' is therefore logically constitutively reinterpreted.)

Vitality, immediacy of consciousness is vitality of movement in the constitutive relationships that is all the richer the more comprehensive the correlativity between the possible determinations and determination unities turns out to be. The concretion grows with the consciousness; provided that consciousness is self-consciousness it has reached the highest and total concretion. The primal concretion consists in the universality of this correlativity being itself conscious in an absolute self-consciousness in its process of relatedness, of the logical emanation from primal instances of lawfulness.[2]

The primordial concrete apprehension of the vitality of the complex of lived experience is nothing other than the thinking of the origin related to the correlativity of the constitution complexes in the correlativity of something objective and something subjective. The relation is a primal-theoretical one, more exactly it is also no longer a relation, but is the process of primal thinking itself in its actuality, i.e. of the infinitely dimensional complex, of the primal dialectic of the constitutive relationships and categories and principles. (Now it becomes understandable: *what* is immobilized by the *description*; which immediacy, which vital, which concrete thing becomes abstract; which stream is immobilized; what *description* is thought to be related to, namely to the *constitution* complex. *Description: objectification.*)

Philosophy has as its goal – which it never reaches, but only persists in striving towards it – this absolute concretion of the relation of consciousness in which every singularization is superseded and only has a sense as singularization of a higher and finally ultimate unity which is that of the absolute and certain knowing, of self-knowing.

Existence and proper ultimate concrete existence is that from where an infinite-fold, infinitely dimensional complex of the lawfulness of constitutive relationships is made possible and realized. Philosophy completes itself as thinking of thinking and thereby attains a unitary problem sphere: consciousness in the correlative counter-directions of objectification and subjectification. That is a problem sphere which – subsumed under the idea of constitution – makes possible a strictly unitary systematics and conceptually grasps and in this way comprehends the all-ness of being and ought, the totality of the world.

To the extent to which the idea of constitution can concern anything and everything, the preconception that is expressed in it proves to be a philosophical one in the usual sense. (Natorp's psychology has the advantage that it determines what is meant by the *irrational*, while the concept of the irrational in Lipps is determined merely from the formal opposition of form and content.)

(c) The radicalization of the theoretical in the idea of constitution

The idea of constitution is 1. radical and 2. universal. Constituted means uniformly determined in consciousness. Every object, every something is determined as something, determined as determined in relationships and in relationships, to the extent to which the latter are part of a unity. Relating and relationship is only another formulation of the essence of consciousness. Therefore the constitution complex is strictly and radically logically grasped, not psychologically or subjectively. Constituted in consciousness does not mean: traced back to conditions of subjectivity as a proper sphere of being, but rather constituted means: being based on and uniformly determined in ultimate logical law complexes.[3]

This logical radicalization of the idea of constitution, its detachment from the idea of the subjective, makes possible the universality of its domain. In this way, it encompasses the subjective itself and in as much as it does so, it encompasses the one and the other, therefore also and exactly the 'and', the correlation, so that now the universality forbids ever again isolating what is objective and what is subjective. Every such isolation means a falling-away from the idea of philosophy.

The radicalization of the idea of constitution is, however, at the same time characterized in a particular way and if we take this into account the preconception itself is thereby determined even more closely.

The constitutive unity of determination is that of primal thinking. Being and consciousness, positing of being and positing of the ought just as everything that is determined in such positings and the process of this determining itself is taken into consideration as subsumed under such ultimate unity.

If one considers everything in such a way, if one, as it were, dedicates oneself to this preconception, then nothing escapes the strict systematics that can be developed from it. Any describing of individual phenomena, each getting caught in concrete individual questions or even any attempt to put something concrete, singularized into the centre of philosophy, is judged from the beginning to be philosophically naive or even as not philosophical; naive because uncritical, uncritical because one does not consider the underlying presuppositions. (One attains a universal, radical, irrefutable, and critical superiority which is certain as long as one takes it seriously!)

Under this preconception everything is subject to presuppositions and there is the possibility that such a philosophy has something like 'depths'. Because one can show that any isolated question, any approach has a background of presuppositions, namely presuppositions of all being, ought, and doing. The preconception makes it possible to let anyone who is philosophically naive know what they are doing insofar as one confronts them with the universality of the infinite relationship complexes of the absolute self-positing self-consciousness.

One would grossly misunderstand the considerations and their goal if one were of the opinion that there was even the intention to prove this preconception to be unmotivated and unjustified or to be 'false'. On the contrary, it should be understood as definitely motivated and the *possibility* of the universal systematics based on it should be fully examined. (The idea of constitution as an expression of a preconception motivated in the emancipation of the theoretical as an attitude.)

The idea of constitution has its motive in an experience of factical life, namely that instances of knowledge and fixations do not endure, that they get disputed, that knowledge, in reflective thinking further, turns out to be dependent on the subject. Implied in the knowing determination, the determination of objects, there is also the tendency towards valid and fixed determination. The task of securing knowledge is motivated in this way, to the extent that it is dependent on the subject; securing implies determination of subjectivity. (Knowing seeks to help itself. History of the not explicit 'theory of knowledge'.)

Implied in the tendency of knowing and in its sense there is a task, to be precise – the task of valid determining of the object – a task that is not

DESTRUCTING CONSIDERATION OF THE NATORPIAN POSITION

tailored to a specific subject but is an open possibility that determines nothing, for a plurality of subjects. Factically, in each case the factical experience of the uncertainty of knowledge is made in the factical lifeworld (environing and with-world).

What is primary is the devotion to a domain of subject matter, consecutively not the boundedness to a specific individual subject. The task holds the relation complex as such together and at the same time it prevents any intrusion of a personal self-worldly moment. As science, this task becomes a public affair, a matter of culture; and to the extent that it objectively gives, for itself, prominence to this task by virtue of its own sense, it also lastingly determines, often in a guiding and directing way, the history of cultures and of spirit. It makes possible a particular way of handing down and inheriting, of tradition, *of attitude*. It keeps public opinion bound to historical culture and always keeps it occupied with it. (It brings a bond with it and in this way feigns a fulfilment of Dasein in the objective achievement. That is cultural idealism. Theory provides typical reference and paradigms for all objectifying achievement!)

This objectivity of the task is accompanied by universality, the fact that it can concern all life experiences. One can even see a cultural task, indeed even the aim of cultural development in the penetration of life by the objectivity and certainty of scientific rational knowledge and can let all vitality and actuality of life derive their sense from there. It concerns a task that is held to be eminently difficult, which however in principle is very easy after all, even if an all-round exact carrying-out of this task may take exception to the peculiarity of life facts that cannot easily be dissolved into pure thinking, even if furthermore the entire apparatus of such theoretical penetration of life, i.e. its normative determination [*Normierung*] of the measure of rational validity of reason in every respect, may not be accessible to everyone straight away.

The task is in principle easy because it enactmentally consists in taking up the theoretical relation of knowledge or in entering into an attitude. In addition to its fundamental ease, it is even seductive because its possible universality – which all the more securely offers itself the more untiringly the attitude is maintained in a self-forgetting way – feigns full validity and finality of the clarification of life, determination and decision. This deception for its part succeeds so uninhibitedly because the attitude and the task given with it is accessible to all – public opinion, the community – and this accessibility is taken as a guarantee for the fact that a decision is taken in this attitude, can be determined as an absolute decision, i.e. can be 'thought to the end' if the attitude is sufficiently radicalized. Life receives its determination from the attitude, becomes a matter-of-fact task and matter of culture. As objective good and inter-subjective availability, task and attitude can be transmitted as a tradition. With the inheritance, the continuation, intensification, improvement and instruction gives itself to ideals (of rationality) which are pre-delineated in the attitude itself. The possibility of being transmitted as a tradition again increases the certainty of the security of this way despite all variation, in terms of content, of the formulation of the task and its solution.

The pure, radical and universal dominance of the idea of constitution in philosophy is the culmination of such a tradition. In it, knowing itself is guaranteed in its universal achievement and simultaneously the predominance of theoretical consciousness within the whole problematic of spirit and reason is maintained. This culmination is already there in German idealism. (The most poignant index for it: that religion has become pure educational and cultural religion [*Bildungsreligion*].) Today, through the progression of a developed exact science (natural and human science) and the logically more exact Kantianism that is thereby nurtured and shaped as well as through the development and enrichment of logic itself, the idea of constitution is itself detached from psychological mixtures and in its lawfulness has simply become more visible. The thinking to the end of this idea can no longer be exceeded, in as much as it is universally posited in such a way that even, 'soul', 'God', 'life' receive their sense only from it.

When we speak of the 'ease' of the attitude here, we do not mean its technical carrying-out, the fulfilment of the conditions and requirements *in* the enactment but rather the approach to enactment itself. The situation of adapting oneself, of entering into the attitude, the attitude itself is devotion to a task, to the matter as matter. The attitude is enactment of a self-world, but precisely such a one that in it the relation is simply unconcerned about the self-world [*selbstweltunbekümmert*]. Attitude is the pushing away [*Wegstellung*] from the self-world. It is easy because it is absolved of the self-worldly worry, absolves itself of it, of a worry that is heavy. This 'ease' and 'heaviness' are specifically self-worldly concepts of Dasein. It is typical for contemporary life and its domination by the theoretical to pass off exactly the scientific and further matter-of-factness as the most difficult, to take the self-worldly worry lightly and to relieve oneself of it by way of being cultivated and knowledgeable, or to not take it seriously at all.

DESTRUCTING CONSIDERATION OF THE NATORPIAN POSITION

The idea of constitution is motivated in the problem of knowledge and is itself supposed to secure the theoretical. If it is taken universally and determines the preconception of philosophy, then philosophy is attitude, i.e. the pushing away from the self-world. It remains this – or more exactly, it merely exceeds itself – if it becomes attitude even to the self-world. It then becomes an exponential pushing away of the latter and every attempt at a concretion, at an immediate apprehension of life and life experience is only attitudinal.

With the preconception of constitution everything – what is objective and what is subjective – is predestined to be a complex of relationships, a subject matter-ness or thingly-ness in the broadest sense. Everything falls victim to this fate. 'God' becomes the absolute *universitas* of these relationships, which, in principle, is absolutely knowable.

To the extent that philosophy has its motive in a self-worldly worry – think of the problem of the a priori – the idea of constitution as preconception of philosophy means the falling-away from the latter itself. Philosophy as attitude is a pushing away from its proper sense. The radicalization of the theoretical in the idea of constitution in principle – also when it is carried out most rigorously – never leads to concrete actual Dasein. The system of the universal logical correlativity manages to pass off the dead as living or to pretend that logically dialectical relationships are the actuality of life. But this is something living for those dead ones who have made it easy for themselves.

The idea of constitution has from the beginning forced every problem of philosophy into a fixed course so that it becomes impossible to let anything *outside the attitude* to enter into the motivation.

The complex of lived experience and the question of its relation of apprehension is predetermined with the idea. It may be absolutely conceded to Natorp that the 'I' cannot be thought as 'I', cannot be an object of thinking. The question is only whether it has to be an object of thinking and whether what it 'is' is determined in thinking. The self-world is, in principle, not to be apprehended in an attitude because attitude is the pushing away from it. And the fact that its sense is seen in that it is the ground and condition of possibility of the pushing away from it itself, drives the theoretical to its extreme and means declining in principle to concede even the mere possibility of a different determination of the origin [*Ursprungsbestimmung*] of the concrete.

Now, whether the idea of constitution is, as is the case of the Marburgers, conceived absolutely logically and one claims the absolute

CONSTITUTION AS GUIDING PRECONCEPTION

logical formation [*Durchgeformtheit*] of the individual or whether an irrational residue is granted to the latter and one says that the pure determinations of form do not add up to the content, is only a secondary distinction. Also in the latter case, the attitude remains, only with resignation. The concept of philosophy is in principle the same; it is self-worldly worried unworried, i.e. a philosophy that by means of its own preconception makes the task impossible for itself – and that is nonetheless a philosophy because the philosophical motive is alive in it. The position is therefore based on an attitudinal preconception in which what it seeks slips through its fingers, precisely because and in as much as it is an attitude.

Therefore – one would have to say by means of argumentation and by philosophizing in words – philosophy should dispense with thinking and abandon itself to enthusing and intuiting. The fact that the specific preconception is made understood as attitudinal and therefore as a non-primordial preconception – the origin-characterization of the enactment of the attitude has to show that even more closely – does not mean that philosophy dispenses with thinking. The question is simply whether the theoretical does not have a more primordial form or a non-attitudinal character. If one manages to primordially understand this possibility then enough is achieved.

However, in this case, the thinking of thinking and the opinion that one thereby satisfies the motive of philosophy must be dispensed with, provided that thinking of thinking means: thinking of consciousness, thinking of what is there in consciousness as being there in the sense of constitution and *thinking of thinking*: following the universal logical complex of constitution.

The preconception determines philosophy as a theoretical attitude, such that especially moments that it has always claimed surely belong to it: universality and adherence to principles. (Attitude: a relation complex subordinate to a universal idea determining the domain of subject matter, in whose sense or structure it itself is co-given such that the character of enactment belonging to it makes a primordial access to the self-world impossible.)

If we want to understand the relation of apprehension that is particular to this position and is determined by the preconception of the same, the radical proof of the all-round inter-relationships of the constitution complexes, then the characterization of enactment and the decision on primordiality cannot be avoided.

DESTRUCTING CONSIDERATION OF THE NATORPIAN POSITION

Such a deliberation will also be accepted as an addition to the considerations; and yet one will not refrain from remarking that such lapsing into the establishing of facts and statements of the factual course is most inappropriate, especially with regard to the position under discussion, since especially here everything enactment like, the actuality, is transposed into the logical categorially dialectical complexes of movement of the constitutional relationships. The philosophy of the Marburgers would in this way be confronted with questions and points of view that are foreign to it. Any determination and decision about it on the basis of this direction of consideration would be external and at bottom unfruitful.

At first, it looks as if this were the case and the difficulty should be admitted, especially since it is based on an argumentation that is grounded in the dominant concept of philosophy. However, it is also impossible to reject the following reminder, as unscientific or even unphilosophical and trivial as it might seem: that philosophy still purports to be something other than mere science, even when and especially where it is confronted with the ideal of strict science. After all a higher status and function is ascribed to it that goes beyond the mere supplying of results of knowledge, already by the fact that philosophical knowledge is supposed to make accessible *what is fundamental* and that which concerns the *whole* of life. (The reminder of the more than mere knowledge in the enactment of philosophy does not solve the problem, it merely gives an occasion to enquire into what is there.)

We include the validity of what is philosophically known towards life, which mostly remains unclear and external (usability for, application to), and correspondingly the direction [*Hinordnung*] of philosophy itself towards and into life in a sense that exceeds mere practical occupation with matters of knowledge. We include them as a motive that at first is not clearly formulated and dijudicated, if we, in spite of the earlier difficulty, pose the question of enactment to a philosophy that turns away from the sphere of enactment. For the question of enactment – 'question' already in the specifically philosophical sense – will prove to fit without rupture and detour into the primordial motives and tendencies of philosophizing. And the universality of the object area and the validity of the proposition as well as the adherence to principles of instances of knowledge will prove to be only the logicized surrogate or the attitudinally fallen away expression of philosophical motives.

Is philosophy something other than a mental exercise [*Denksport*] that is not bound to a subject matter? And something other than an aestheticizing image making and system making of the universe and the human being? Is the relatedness of philosophy to actual life more than that of erudition, of acumen and witty tingly fraying? And is this relatedness more than an always belated assurance that what is known should be valid for life? Is the enquiring in philosophy not an occupation with life set apart from actual life? Then in the end the question of enactment cannot be merely a question of opinion and supplementation as it might still seem at first sight. (The problem of lived experience is articulated through the four earlier questions. If we keep our eye on the question of enactment, it turns out that it is co-determined with this problem up to a certain point, indeed that it only has the function of leading us to the question of enactment so that the latter is sure to pose itself only in the destruction of the problem of lived experience.)

(d) Enactmental and order-complex

[Transcript: Oskar Becker]

The consideration of the primordiality of an enactmental complex already presupposes a criterion for primordiality. Concrete self-worldly Dasein serves as a measure. However, one cannot form a *schema* with which to approach every problem. Nevertheless, we must become clear about what enactment means.

Enactment and enacting is an occurrence. Complexes of lived experience enact themselves: 'I thought about something', 'I gave something a lot of thought.' The complex of considerations of lived experience of some kind enacted itself. The lived experience is integrated into a whole. This enactmental complex into which the lived experience is being integrated can be conceived in a broader or narrower sense. Certain deliberations can arise 'now', 'in this place' (several simultaneously at various places in the lecture hall). No objective complex of nature is needed for this. Lived experiences occur in the environing world and in the temporal sequence of the environmental happening. The lived experiences that now enacted themselves belong each time to a closed complex of lived experience. Between different complexes of that kind (i.e. the mental life of various persons), there is an unbridgeable chasm. In spite of reciprocal understanding, those complexes of lived experience never flow together but are separated from one another by an absolute chasm. (James calls it the greatest chasm in nature.)

DESTRUCTING CONSIDERATION OF THE NATORPIAN POSITION

Individual enactments occur in one's own complex of lived experience. This, however, is still ambiguous. 1. It can mean: The lived experience as an actual one has a unity by virtue of belonging to an 'I' that enacts it. 2. This complex of lived experience can be considered in its completeness, provided that it occurs at all in a consciousness. (Natorp's existence of lived experience in a supra-temporal consciousness.) Everywhere, however, lived experience occurs in an order complex. Also the belongingness to the 'I' is a certain order complex. The order complexes into which the occurring of lived experiences is inserted are probably, in terms of content, different according to individual determinations of the relation of order, but the relation of order is in principle the same. If lived experience is comprehended as existence, 'happening' in any arbitrary area, then the sense of the enactment is already theoretically objectified. As a result, the way to the complex of enactment is obstructed. As soon as enactment is conceived as happening in a relation of order, the proper sense of the enactmental is cut off at the outset.

Earlier we erected a criterion of primordiality: that in the sense of the enactment lay the requirement for a renewal that would co-constitute self-worldly Dasein. That was, however, still an environing worldly and not a purely primordial characterization. Does this criterion itself not have the same character as an order complex? (Is not the 'experiencing oneself', the 'making of self-worldly Dasein' etc. an order complex?) This question is decisive and can only be solved step by step; it must above all be concretely specified.

(For the carrying-out of the solution, we wanted to consider James, Münsterberg and Dilthey; due to lack of space, we have to restrict ourselves to Dilthey and can only dedicate a few comments to James and Münsterberg.)

In order to identify Dilthey's position, we will choose a form of presentation that is different from the one we used for Natorp. The guiding questions of the destruction remain the same but in Dilthey they assume a different ordering, although also in him the idea of constitution plays a part.

SECTION TWO
The destructing consideration of the Diltheyian position

[Transcript: Oskar Becker]

§ 16 The attitudinal character of Natorp's philosophy and the expectation of the opposite in Dilthey's

Natorp and Dilthey occupy two sharply opposing positions. First, we present Dilthey as if there were no essential difference between him and Natorp at all, in order to then let the opposition between the two come all the more to the fore. This is difficult, however, because one usually inserts Dilthey into the conventional schema of contemporary philosophy. At the same time we therewith bring the characterization of enactment of the Natorpian philosophy to a conclusion.

It is clear that the question about the enactment of the philosophical attitude is foreign to Natorp's philosophy and appears to do it injustice. However, if we grasp the idea of constitution *radically*, we can nevertheless pose the question. According to Natorp, the question of enactment is a separate question that is not philosophically motivated. However, in every philosophy *more* is claimed than in mere science and this 'more' leads back to the motive of philosophizing itself. No philosophy is shielded from this question about the motive, least of all one with claims to strict scientific rigour.

In philosophy, knowledge, knowledge of principles is sought and therewith that which becomes known shall not merely become known but shall also have a final meaning for the whole of life. If philosophy is more than mere thinking about life that is bound to subject matter, more than 'getting an idea of it', than setting up a system, if one requires more than the external relationship to life that consists in the fact that what is known should be 'valid' for life (as norm); then the question about the enactment of philosophizing is no mere question of knowledge but a question regarding principles.

One mostly associates the enactmental with the idea of the 'flow' in factical occurring. But this is mistaken. It becomes apparent in the history of psychology that at first the enactmental is taken from *environing worldly* occurring, as given in the world, just as one factically comprehends it, although this attitude of enactment was never *thoroughly* grasped in the environing world. It is rather that one grasped the 'world' straight away as the 'whole of nature', neither as environing world nor as world of physical objectivity in the strict sense. From this arises the idea to posit the enactment in a marked-off sphere of a self-contained individual. The complexes of lived experience of the individuals are in reality separated. Such a complex of lived experience can be conceived 1. as real psychical occurring, 2. as something that carries a *sense* in itself, that means something (as complex of intentionalities). The enactmental complex is somehow centred in the concrete 'I' who resides in the lived experiences. The 'I' is the unity of the stream of lived experience. If one formulates it even more precisely as pervaded by a certain structure, determined by a particular lawfulness, it proves to be a singular instance of a typical ('eidetic') complex of lived experience. One can ask from where the stream of lived experience receives its ultimate lawfulness. One answers: from a 'pure "I"' from which the *typical* relations of the stream become understandable. One can go still further and find the ultimate sense of the stream of lived experience in a pure temporality (Husserl's 'primordial phenomenological time'). Therefore, there are various orderings in the stream of lived experience and in them a specific sense of order complex is determined. These different order complexes distinguish themselves in terms of content (as order in the world and in the different unities of lived experience). But this difference between the orders is no ultimate, fundamental one because even the classification into the ultimate time of consciousness [*Bewußtseinszeit*] is a classification into an order complex in which the lived experiences belong to an 'I' that forms the unity of the complex of lived experience. This unity-forming 'I' plays a role in every order complex. (Natorp denies that time presents an ultimate order that was instead to be found in a supra-temporal context.)

ATTITUDINAL CHARACTER OF NATORP'S PHILOSOPHY

In this connection, one starts out from an undetermined concept of occurring that is taken from the environing world. This concept of occurring receives the character of an uppermost genus; *all* occurring is mere determination of this concept of occurring. That is because since Plato philosophy is epistemically attuned, in fact, in a double sense. Philosophy has the character of a task of gaining knowledge, not only that philosophy is *absolute* knowledge but also that *all* genuine life-worlds are, according to their relation, determined from the *theoretical* relation. Philosophy itself is theoretical attitude and that whereupon philosophy attunes itself is (mostly unknowingly) pre-determined through the theoretical form of life.

Let us apply this consideration to Natorp: The idea of constitution brings everything into *one* order complex. Is this idea insufficient? Our previous criterion of primordiality is certainly still provisional. (It consisted of two moments: 1. the enactment should be self-worldly directed, 2. should, according to its sense, require a renewal that co-constitutes self-worldly Dasein.)

The Natorpian philosophy's relation of apprehension is the tracing into the constitution complexes. It leads to an absolute dialectic. (It does contain a division due to the two directions of object determining, the objectifying and subjectifying one, but this opposition is superseded in the universal primal logic.)

Is this relation of apprehension that aims at the ultimate constitution not self-worldly directed? Does it not refer to the self, to consciousness? No, this relation of apprehension never aims at the concrete self-world, everything only has sense with regard to the external constitution complex. (The concrete self is, according to Natorp, 'neither the first nor the last'.[1]) The 1. moment of the criterion of primordiality is therefore not fulfilled. This is rather the case with the 2. moment. Natorp constantly emphasizes that knowledge never reaches the end but is always under way, always in the infinite progress of determination. One could see in that the necessity of a constant renewal of the enactmental complex. However, this Natorpian progress towards the infinite, this constant renewal does not in any way co-constitute self-worldly, actual Dasein, but exactly gives it up. It is not only that this process is theoretical and does not allow the self-world to come into action, but it is not at all thought as really enacted in history, it is rather that this infinite 'fieri' of the λόγος is to be thought as the absolute dialectical process of the absolute self-consciousness. In no way is the enactment such that it constitutes the actual Dasein of a concrete individual.

DESTRUCTING CONSIDERATION OF THE DILTHEYIAN POSITION

Therefore, under the presupposition – we must draw attention especially to this – that the criterion of primordiality in use can be justified from the genuine motive of philosophy, the Natorpian philosophy is *not* primordial but has fallen away into an attitudinal character. We confront the Natorpian standpoint with a completely different one, that of Dilthey.

One has inserted Dilthey into the schema of contemporary philosophy. One says his philosophy refers to the special relation between natural and human sciences and that he had concretely opened new horizons for the human sciences. But that he had not been a proper philosopher; that he could not formulate his investigations in concepts, that he did not succeed in establishing a systematic connection between them. One sees in him a great historian but denies his primordially creative philosophical achievement. One says that in an historical manner of consideration he had sought a replacement for a system that he had not been granted to create.

This understanding of Dilthey is the common one and it is not totally unjustified. Rather, one must characterize him in such a way if one approaches his philosophy from the outside. However, where nowadays it is the habit of seeing Dilthey's *limits*, therein lies, according to our understanding, exactly his strength. It is not that Dilthey *could* not have come to a conceptual formulation but until the end he *shied away* from a systematic conclusion. (Only towards the end of his life did he demonstrate systematic aspirations.) However, Dilthey did not determine the concept of philosophy from out of its proper motive.

In our presentation we will first bring out the features in Dilthey that are related to those of contemporary philosophy. Seen from the outside it looks as if Dilthey had only wanted to offer a laying of the ground of the human sciences. According to him, the human sciences have the goal of objectively portraying the spiritual connections between human history and culture. We are searching for a theory of these sciences. We now have no general theory of science at all. We must therefore proceed from the human sciences themselves. However, in order to guard ourselves against one-sidedness we must choose their concept as comprehensively as possible. In the area of human sciences, there is as a task not only the knowing about knowledge but also about the value and about the purposes (about giving rules), about religious belief etc. All life is pervaded by life's reflections on its own positings: thereby it is shaken, drawn into doubt. From there arises the tendency towards a secure knowledge; the highpoint of this tendency is philosophy; it is the consciousness of consciousness, the knowledge about knowledge (note the similarity with Natorp's formulations!). Provided that the philosopher wants to stabilize the whole of life he moves onto the same level as the religious prophet and the poet. They all stand in a region detached from life from which they seek to *be normative for* life. That is just like in transcendental philosophy.

However, in his last work ('The Construction of the Historical World in the Human Sciences') Dilthey abandoned this standpoint again. He says that ultimately the historical *limitedness* becomes evident in the philosophically absolute positings. It is questionable whether all of these positings can ultimately be traced back to something that is unconditioned. This question cannot be decided with certainty. At the end of his life, after a temporary lapse into transcendental philosophy, Dilthey has again found himself with this perspective.

The problem of the human sciences is not a separate problem but the expression of an ultimate philosophical motive: to interpret life from out of itself, primordially.

Life philosophy is for us a necessary station on the way of philosophy, in contrast to empty formal transcendental philosophy. One subsumes Dilthey under the concept of historicism and fears in him the specter of relativism; but we must lose the fear of this specter.

We insert here an index of Dilthey's most important writings:

1. *The Life of Schleiermacher.* I. vol. 1870. II. vol. (from the *Nachlaß*; in production)
2. *Introduction to the Human Sciences.* I. 1883
3. 'The Poet's Creation'[2] (in the *Zeller-Festschrift*) 1887
4. 'On the Problem of the Origin of the Belief in the Reality of the External World' 1890 (*Berliner Berichte*)
5. 'The Idea of a Descriptive and Analytic Psychology' 1894 (*Berliner Berichte*)
6. 'Contributions to the Study of Individuality' 1896 (*Berliner Berichte*)
7. 'The Origin of Hermeneutics' (*Sigwart-Festschrift*) 1900
8. 'On the Function of Anthropology' 1904 (*Berliner Berichte*)
9. 'Studies on the Laying of the Ground for the Human Sciences.' I. 1905 (*Berliner Berichte*)
10. *Experience and Poetry.* Leipzig 1905
11. 'On the Essence of Philosophy.' (*Kultur der Gegenwart*, section on Systematic Philosophy)

12. 'The Construction of the Historical World in the Human Sciences.' (Essays of the Royal Prussian Academy.) 1910
13. 'The Types of Worldviews.' (Anthology 'Worldview' edited by Frischeisen-Köhler.) 1911
14. *Collected Writings* II. vol. Leipzig 1914 (contains critical work). Essays here and there in the *Archiv für Geschichte der Philosophie*, in the *Deutsche Rundschau* etc.

§ 17 Report on Dilthey's philosophy

Dilthey intended to give a critique of historical reason, as a supplement to Kant, which was not even achieved by neo-Kantianism. He is guided – as transcendental philosophy is – by the tendency towards the laying of the ground of objectivity. He also takes into consideration the grounding of the natural sciences. However, the complexes of values must also be secured in themselves if one wants to ground objectivity. (The impetus for the formation of the Windelband-Rickertian philosophy of value departed from here.) The task of the hierarchy of values emerges, of the securing of the norm complexes, as they grow from the determinations of aims as rule giving. This is not foreign to philosophy. Philosophy is the thoughtful securing and clarification of life itself. It is only a continuation of life reflection and its securing against the doubts of life. Thinking is at its highpoint the knowledge of knowledge, consciousness of consciousness. Here Dilthey appends the meaningful sentence: 'Thinking is bound to life through an inner necessity, it is itself a form of life.'[1] The task of philosophy is therefore: laying of the ground, summarizing, generalization; reflection [*Besinnung*] on the ground, purpose, value of life. (Here the epistemological task is still unconnectedly set next to the task of worldview; they are only held together through the reflection on themselves.) Provided that the philosopher is brought out with regard to life and has an eternal order before him, he is related to the poet or the religious person. They, too, want to lend support to life. Philosophy and religion thus have the same tendency and for this reason the most incisive oppositions arise between them, between the rationality of philosophy and the irrationality of religion.

Thinking is at first knowledge-according in the human sciences that understand life. Every word, every act is only understood in that the person expressing them shares a common ground with the one who understands (what we now call 'empathy'). Everything that arose historically carries the label of the common ground on it. All objectivity is furthermore embedded into the complex of nature. The objective is the effected, created. However, the objectivities nevertheless retain their effectiveness, even if they are exposited from life and therewith remain in life. We have in it a proper teleological complex (in their comprehension, positing of values, purpose -giving.) These complexes are not yet the most comprehensive forms. They are encompassed by the spiritual complex of a generation, an epoch or an age that determine the having-become whole of life. (Spengler's basic thought is already present here.) Dilthey calls this the *effecive complex* of an epoch etc. This is the fundamental concept of the human sciences: from here the historical and systematic human sciences subdivide. The human science has to determine and systematically extend what is norm giving. The whole of the world serves as a background for the concrete historical comprehension. In this way, there exists a constant correlativity between historical and systematic human sciences.

What is the core, the primal element of the effective complex? The actual primal cell is the individual, the unity of life, provided that it lives in its milieu. In this way, emerges the task of a general structural theory of the unity of life. These are regarded in view of the typical as detached from their facticity. Psychology investigates these structural complexes. They are not disclosed but are given in the unities of life themselves, they are lived in the pre-theoretical. In this respect, they can be accessed by description and immediate analysis. In this way, emerges the idea of a 'descriptive and analytic psychology' or a 'structural psychology'. Its tasks are: 1. to give *cross-sections* of mental life; 2. to present *longitudinal sections*: general biography; 3. determination and securing of what results from the context: the acquired complex of mental life. (One sees here a gradual growing of the Diltheyian concepts that are discovered from out of the concrete.) This is the *status conscientiae*, the immobilized state of consciousness, which is compared to another one. It is characterized through representations, processes of feeling and willing. However, in each of these moments the other one is also encountered. It is not about a quantitative predominance of one factor, but the inner relationship of the complexes of lived experience shows various kinds of structure that is unitarily pervaded by a specific sense. The whole of the complex of lived experience is a whole of processes. Everything psychical is a process. The only thing that is completely permanent in this process is the self in its correlative relationship to the milieu (which is reciprocal). (Here lie still today valuable preconceptions, *especially in the essay about the belief in the reality of the external world* that at that time was struck down by neo-Kantianism. Only Scheler made use of them. Dilthey's historical works are also important here.)

This correlative relationship of self and milieu must be primordial and may not be theoretically conceived. Dilthey interprets it as the self's experience of resistance: it encounters a resistance of a living and not dead character. We are not criticizing this comprehension here; we only understand it as impetus for what Dilthey calls the development of the life complex.

We must still make some remarks on the *status conscientiae*. The three elements representation, feeling, willing process are always contained in a state of consciousness. Representation is the intentional content, that whereupon, for example, the will is directed. Feeling is not a conglomerate of sensations of pleasure and displeasure. The sting of a wound e.g. is a special kind of reality. (Here Dilthey saw the right thing, even if still in a rough manner.) By the term feeling must also be understood approving and disapproving, liking and disliking and interest in something. Interest is the part in the 'I' that springs from the milieu. One could have doubts about seeing a feeling in a pure sensation, e.g. a colour. However, already Goethe made the remarkable observation that a landscape, viewed through coloured glasses, displays different moods. Clearer still are the moods that accompany different sounds. Also thought like processes are linked with particular feelings, like evidence with a sense of wellbeing and contradiction with a sense of discomfort. According to Dilthey, the volitional moments of a state of consciousness are not everywhere verifiable. Every feeling does press towards intensification or repression and therefore has a tendency. And also the course of a chain of associations shows a certain direction as tendency; but nevertheless, according to Dilthey, the question must remain open.

Through the predominance of one of the three moments a certain state of consciousness is identified as representation (thinking), feeling or will. However, the difference lies above all in a changing inner relationship of the elements among one another.

Two lines of development are to be distinguished in the mental: one *according to thought*: from the sensations via the associations etc. to the process of thinking. This goes in the direction from milieu to the self. The other *according to will*: the motive under which the self decides itself ... action. Direction: from the self to the milieu. How can those two contrarily directed basic lines be united, how do they stand in the whole of the complex of lived experience? They must be regarded with respect to the *value* they have for the whole of the complex of lived experience. If consciousness were only representational consciousness, there would be no causal relationship between the self and the milieu. (Here there is present in Dilthey a mixture of phenomenological and natural-scientific – psycho-physiological – concepts, like stimulus etc.) Consciousness would then be immobile and dead because an action is only initiated through motives, through values that are felt. Experiencing itself becomes a possible motive for an action. The ultimate self is, in its core, drive and feeling. What results is a bundle of feelings and drives as ultimate centre.

How does the effective complex of the mental life relate to this? The structural complex is: 1. in each of its moments unitarily there; 2. it stands in relationship to the milieu: adaptation (which is *no* biological-natural-scientific category); 3. the sequence of lived experiences can never be determined through the principle of *causality*: *causa aequat effectum*. No representation etc. is sufficient ground for another one. We never know where we are going.

How about the 'longitudinal section' (the biography)? Which fundamental elements determine the developmental complex of a life? (Concerning this, one must especially compare the concrete biographies of Schleiermacher, Hegel, Novalis, Hölderlin etc.) With regard to a biography, one must proceed from the brightly illuminated stages, not from dark beginnings and reconstruct the development from there. One may not put forward any hypotheses but everything must immanently lie in the complex of lived experience, also the goal of the development. All mental development takes its course in a milieu, it consists in an attaining of values, it receives in its course an *articulation*; in this way the *acquired* life complex finally forms itself. The mental complex tends to bring each state of consciousness to its highest possible fulfilment. For the thought-according, feeling-according and will-according complex different particular characteristics are possible: self-control with regard to will, purity with regard to feeling etc. with a tendency towards an absolute harmonic form *of the soul*. There is thus a subjective purposiveness that points towards an absolute life ideal. (Reference to Goethe.) The formal structure of the life complex is thus for Dilthey ultimately determined by the ideal of humanity of Goethe and Humboldt. Through this articulation the life complex solidifies, it becomes the fixed possession of the person; all living experience of the person must be determined in this

DESTRUCTING CONSIDERATION OF THE DILTHEYIAN POSITION

acquired complex. It is the basis for the problem of individuation. In this lies the focal point of the human sciences, however, the general developmental complex stands in the background. Towards the end of Dilthey's *Introduction to the Human Sciences*, there is the following sentence: 'We must insist on making the abundance of the life of the soul accessible to us in an unbiased way.' The comprehension of mental life must be a *primordial* one. It may not be detached, it has to question its objects and its objecthoods itself. However, the (formal) logical fundamental concepts are also valid for mental life. Mental life becomes accessible in *inner perception*. The latter is no set apart isolated act of reflection. Dilthey sees the problem of inner perception not in whether it had evidence or certainty or which scope belonged to it. (For Dilthey, who considered everything as an historian, inner perception does not have that absolute evidence that phenomenologists most of the time attribute to it.) Rather, he considers the abundance of its structure. According to Dilthey inner perception has an inner intellectuality, it is pervaded by an inner conceptuality. The general forms of thinking, the formal achievements of dividing, connecting, linking etc. have the task of elucidating the mental complex, but in such a way that what is elucidated *remains* in the mental complex. The discursive forms of thinking have the task of *depiction*, judgment and conclusion the task of supporting. Dilthey did not make this inner intellectuality of inner perception into a problem. The inner intuition must for itself always bring everything to givenness in the whole of the acquired complex; all mental meaningfulness can always only be interpreted from the complex, never in an isolated way. Every mental lived experience carries with it a knowledge of its own value. Every living person lives in a feeling itself in which it objectively has the value or un-value of its own Dasein. Every lived experience has this accentuation of value and un-value in the mental complex. This accentuation of value is the guideline for the reconstruction on the model of what is given in the inner intuition. Genuine psychology concretely accompanies this, it stands in relation with the self-world; the psychological is nothing other than the explication of self-worldly experience.

Dilthey did not carry out these approaches. However, provided that one really grasps the problem of lived experience primordially one must see in here an instruction that is not yet exhausted. The thoughts just presented are contained in Dilthey's treatises 'Ideas Concerning a Descriptive and Analytic Psychology' (1894) and 'Studies in Laying the Ground for the Human Sciences' (1905).

In the second text, Dilthey calls attention to Husserl's *Logical Investigations* (1900/01). One cannot esteem this highly enough because at that time (1905) one saw in the actually important and positive second volume of the *Investigations* in general a 'falling back' into the psychologism that was fought against in the first. Dilthey now attempted to bring his psychology into line with the phenomenological results of the *Logical Investigations*. However, he constantly shied away from introducing a new conceptuality. Therefore, due to this more external adoption of Husserlian thought, nothing is actually furthered in him. Dilthey then, for his part, had an effect on Husserl, especially with regard to the problem of nature and spirit, the understanding of culture etc. (Natorp and Dilthey both stand in a particular relationship to Husserl, the influences of which have not yet been settled in Husserl.)

§ 18 The destruction of the Diltheyian philosophy

We must now try to understand Dilthey's preconception; we must see whether it is primordial, to what extent he can pose the question of primordial explication, to what extent his concepts are unitarily pervaded or whether they perhaps do not merely stand unconnected next to the vital feeling of what he has seen.

Three moments are characteristic of Dilthey's understanding of the relational character of inner perception:

1. *Its inner intellectuality*. The 'logical processes' cannot be detached from the inner perception, it articulates itself in itself, lived experience as such already has a certain rationality. Dilthey indeed already thinks lived experience as understanding. One can object that lived experience is made up like a construction. With the 'intellectuality of the inner perception' the problem is only posed but not solved.
2. I experience myself from out of the *whole of a situation*. However, Dilthey interprets this complex too much in terms of comprehension.
3. What is accessible to me has in itself a certain *importance* or *unimportance*, a certain *value* or *unvalued character*. This can provide a guideline for an analysis of the life complex.

Summarizing those three points, it can be shown that psychological thinking grows out of life experience. The latter determines its structure in a process from out of itself. (Here Dilthey only gives, as perhaps every

DESTRUCTING CONSIDERATION OF THE DILTHEYIAN POSITION

great philosopher, intimations: he sees a new reality but the expansion on what is seen is mostly never enacted.)

Let us now subject the Diltheyian philosophy to *destruction*. In Natorp's case we based it on four questions:

1. How is the complex of lived experience intended as a whole?
2. What is the unitary and manifoldness character of the complex of lived experience?
3. How does the 'I' stand with respect to the complex of lived experience?
4. How does the 'I' have itself?

Does this formulation of the questions already have a *primordial* character? This is to be investigated. The destruction of the problem of lived experience is only *one* side of our methodological-critical consideration. We had *singled out* from the problem of *life in general* the *problem of lived experience*, on the one hand, and the *a priori-problem*, on the other. Is this *singling out* acceptable at all?

A remark on Rickert's most recent fight against life philosophy should be included. Seen from his transcendental-philosophical standpoint, Rickert is absolutely consistent, however, from this standpoint he does not see the powers and possibilities of life philosophy.

When destructing the first type (Natorp) we saw that the 'I' takes up a *secondary* position (namely the concrete 'I'; for him the pure 'I' is the problem ground and not at all a problem); the 'I' disappears in the whole of the constitution complex. In Dilthey, the 'I' is, in contrast, the 'primal cell' of the 'effective complex.'(This comparison looks schematic; if we could have also considered Münsterberg and James, i.e. the problems of the *self-positioning* of consciousness and the *stream of consciousness*, our going back to the origin could have been carried out much more concretely.)

Dilthey stands in radical opposition to Natorp. If someone like Natorp, as we saw, is absolutely distant from the origin, we will have to expect that Dilthey is close to the origin.

When destructing Dilthey we must proceed from the *second* of our four viewpoints (questions) (from the manifoldness character of the complex of lived experience). The concept of the *complex* (structural complex, acquired complex, effective complex) is fundamental in Dilthey. The whole of living experience is an effective complex. Lived experience has the basic character of a reality. In the transcendental philosophical sense it is something 'objectified', whereas Natorp understands it as something 'subjectified'. For transcendental philosophy the effective complex is an unphilosophical object because transcendental philosophy is only concerned with constitution. One can argue away all life philosophy by saying that life reality is an objectivity and therefore not psychical (but reified in an unacceptable manner).

One indeed has to ask: Is the transcendental-philosophical position justified in itself or is it capable of interpreting life for itself? Rickert designates being as something that does not contain sense. According to him, figurations of sense are necessarily figurations of value. However, mental reality is a fundamental reality that cannot be judged on the basis of Kantian transcendental philosophy. It perhaps sounds interesting when Rickert fights against intuitionism and characterizes it as the *pathos of laziness*, but it is more difficult to grapple with life than it is to deal with the world in terms of a system. Dilthey attempts to understand the entire world on the basis of life. But he does not succeed because the moment of *constitution* also creeps its way into his philosophy.

The complex of lived experience is seen in such a way that its particular structures become clear as the *condition of the possibility* of understanding the life unity. The effective complex contains that which makes possible the unity of life. Every complex has a functional value as the condition of possibility for interpreting or understanding life. The effective complex as condition for understanding runs through Dilthey's entire psychological considerations. If he wants to determine the ultimate core of psychical unity, he says: the human being is at first primordially a bundle of feeling and drives; the powers of will, the need, the satisfaction are the elementary mental powers. With this, however, mental reality is constructed in a circumstantial, objective, and thingly way. Therefore, the order of constitution stands next to the order of the development of the reality of lived experience from the libidinal centre. These two orders determine the reality of lived experience of the whole of lived experience. One can easily say: that is psychologism or biologism. (Especially if one thinks of the concept of 'adaptation'. Here Dilthey is influenced by James.) What is primordial in Dilthey's tendencies, however, is not biological.

How is the mental itself, the 'I' as 'I' experienced? Living experience is itself a pre-form of understanding (in the manner of historical understanding). The human sciences are only an elaboration of factical life experience. From the outset life has the character of an understanding. Life is 1. effective complex, no logical, dialectical relationship; 2. the complex of lived experience is an historical complex. It stands in a development, it carries in itself an articulation and rationality. Life can be interpreted from out of itself.

From where is the fundamental comprehension of life in Dilthey motivated? Dilthey arrives at mental reality not via an epistemology but by way of consideration and research regarding intellectual history. The effort to understand mental reality in the great concrete figures determines his psychology. From there the concept of understanding is determined for him. In this already lies a danger. It becomes understandable for us if we attempt, leaving aside the transcendental-philosophical influences, to investigate the 'primordial' moments of his position for their ultimate primordiality.

(The emphasis on Dilthey's primordially driving motive or preconception could appear forceful and be taken as a one-sided interpretation of his philosophy. However, one must consider his entire work, not separate opposing statements. As e.g. his praise of 18th-century philosophy, that it lifted the unconscious into the clear light of reason.)

In how far is the understanding's relation of apprehension not primordial? What arises as concrete mental understanding? How is the mental complex meant as understanding? The effective complex is circumstantial, the life complex runs its course in time. This is a circumstantial comprehension of the mental; also in the humanity ideal of a harmonic form of the soul this pull to see a mental complex circumstantially and objectively is only intensified. Dilthey sees the mental only from the outside, although not from the exterior of nature but from the exterior of intellectual history, as a *form*, circumstantially, 'aesthetic' (the ideal of harmony). On the basis of this, he interprets mental reality, from there comes his concept of 'complex'. All this is determined from the aesthetic, form-like apprehension of life. There exists in his work the tendency towards formal harmony; from this preview the individual determination is to be explained. In this manner also a moment of consciousness is determined (as *status conscientiae* through representation, feeling and willing process that are present there together). The self that holds together the unity of the mental only plays the role of the driving forces, of the impulse for the development. Ultimately, the core of the mental lies in the bundle of drives. In this way, it turns out that, despite all tendency towards life reality as a particular one, a circumstantial comprehension after all comes into play. (With regard to this, Dilthey also says that a lot of findings of the previous – 'explanatory' natural-scientific – psychology could be adopted in the new – descriptive and analytic – psychology.) Dilthey is himself unclear about the new towards which he strives. He does not see that only a radicalism that makes all concepts questionable can lead further. The entire conceptual material must be newly determined in primordial apprehension. That is the particular tendency of phenomenology.

§ 19 Natorp and Dilthey – the task of philosophy

We have considered the problem of lived experience from two typical positions, that of Natorp and that of Dilthey. Natorp and Dilthey attempt to understand the complex of lived experience as a whole; as a complex that is determined from the whole, which is pervaded by a primordial unity. But the manner in which the individual is determined from the whole is different in both philosophers. In Natorp, it concerns the whole of the relationship of constitution; in Dilthey, the effective complex of life. In Natorp, it cannot be apprehended in an objectifying way but requires the method of reconstruction. In Dilthey, it is no concept of law but requires primordial explication. In Natorp, there is the opposition between objectification and subjectification; in Dilthey, that between nature complexes and spiritual complexes. According to Natorp, Dilthey's complexes fall within the objectified. Up to a certain degree, the method is the same in both. Natorp's method is *reconstruction*; only that can be reconstructed which previously was constructed. Dilthey's method is the 'constitution' in the complex of life: Only that can be understood that in life and from out of life has uttered itself; life becomes accessible only in its objectifications. In the subsequent understanding of those, primordial life itself is attained. The complex of reconstruction in Natorp is, however, merely formal; in Dilthey, by contrast, it is determined through the connection between lived experience, expression and understanding. Lived experience leads to expression, the latter to understanding, and understanding back to lived experience; in this way it comes full circle.

* * *

What is now the goal of our entire problematic? The problem of lived experience in this singled out form is only singled out on the basis of historically pre-given motives; on the basis of the meaning that life itself has. The problem of life concerns us insofar as we pose the question in

DESTRUCTING CONSIDERATION OF THE DILTHEYIAN POSITION

which way philosophical knowledge explicates itself. The problem of philosophical concept formation is not of a belated nature that pertains to the theory of science; it is the philosophical problem in its origin. It is the problem of attaining the philosophical experience; it explicates the manner of philosophical experiencing.

During the destruction of the two problem groups of the concept of life (the problem of the a priori and of lived experience) a negative result arose: that in both of them the actual self-world, the historically enacted Dasein of each individual as individual disappears, that the self therefore is secondary in every problematic, as (on the one hand, in Natorp) the × of the universal complex of determination; (on the other hand, in Dilthey) as the absolute form of the harmonic soul.

The actual self-world relation plays no primordial role. From the destruction of the a priori problem it followed that transcendental philosophy goes on securely when forgetting the *unum necessarium*, the actual Dasein. At the end of the destruction of the a priori problem the hope remained that the lived experience problem would bring the self-world into the centre of the problematic. (Think of the interest in the 'I' in modern philosophy from Descartes to Dilthey.) But also here where the mental itself is made into a problem, the actual self-worldly Dasein is made into the concrete case of a general, circumstantial constitution complex. Actual Dasein does not come to its primordial due.

Actual Dasein does not become a possible problem. The possibility [of the question] about the novelty of a mental reality is cut off. (Although Dilthey was after all directed towards this.) The reason for this lies in the fact that the primordial motive of philosophy was forgotten and is no longer taken up in the task of philosophy, that instead a lapse into an 'attitude' takes place, a cultivation of certain tasks of gaining knowledge, a tendency towards knowledge (in the theoretical sense), towards ultimate apprehension. Insofar as the philosophical motive is not entirely forgotten, the tendency of philosophy remains towards worldview. Science as a theoretical attitude is of such a nature that it, according to its own sense, puts self-worldly concretion of actual Dasein to the side. As far as philosophy becomes an object of science it is merely objectified. Philosophy cannot be science, it may not lapse into the attitudinal determination. Philosophizing lies before the turn into attitude and before the shaping of experience into the tasks of theoretical research. No more than philosophy has to provide a worldview as a cultivated phenomenon that one can put forward. Philosophy, provided that it remains true to itself, is not meant to rescue or redeem the times, the world etc. or to ease the misery of the masses or to make human beings happy or to form and enhance culture. This all signifies the direction of a worry in which that which matters disappears. All worldview philosophy spoils the primordial motive of all philosophizing. Scientific philosophy is not the science of the kinds of worldview or a systematic of reason as a task that can be handed down or a description of consciousness because that is a circumstantial manner of observation.

In this way, only *negations* arise from our problems, it is a constant nay saying. It would be a misunderstanding to now expect a big 'yes' in the end. The destruction is rather continued; it simply does not have a bad aftertaste. It is the expression of philosophy, provided that in the motive of philosophy lies the securing, or rather, the making insecure, of one's own Dasein. In this continuation of the destruction from out of the tendency to attain and primordially determine the primordial, one is led to primordially and radically grasp the idea of phenomenology, also to understand the non-external, because the understanding of the phenomenological basic posture shows that in it the primordial motives of philosophizing itself can be brought to life.

The questions about intuition and about expression are therefore to be understood in the following way: It is the question about the how of philosophical experience and about the how in which philosophical experience explicates itself, about the motive and the tendency of philosophical experience itself. From this arises the task to secure the employed means and ways in which we approach the origin; in this the particular characteristic of philosophical concepts is expressed.

Philosophy is no attitude towards a content that is apprehended in the enactment of philosophizing, no domain of subject matter that represents an objective complex, no objecthood in a theoretical relation whose enactment character is only at hand but is not seriously considered. The rationality of philosophy will only implicitly come to its due, however, it will not split off but will merely be an immanent illumination of life experience itself that remains in this experience itself and does not step out and turn it into objectivity. Philosophy is pervaded by a fundamental experience that constantly renews itself so that rationality is itself given in this fundamental experience and must form itself in it in terms of content. Therefore there are no philosophical disciplines (such as logic, ethics, aesthetics, philosophy of religion). This division into disciplines is to be reversed. Critical research shows philosophy is to be understood entirely

DESTRUCTING CONSIDERATION OF THE DILTHEYIAN POSITION

historically, centred around the ideal of a humanity. Philosophy does not know any such disciplines. That would mean that its experiencing would dissolve and domains of subject matter would then be standing there. This danger of lapsing into pure reification must constantly be prevented. Therein lies an instruction to ask whether the methodological means and the viewpoints of the destruction are not themselves detached from concrete Dasein, i.e. in terms of subject matter. The four viewpoints of destruction are directed towards a marking off (unity, manifoldness, 'I', 'I' in the complex of the whole etc.). Lived experience is meant as circumstantial objectivity, as domain of subject matter. The four viewpoints of the destruction are conceived formally, however, and prejudge nothing. However, the fact that the formal indication does not prejudge anything does not allow us to content ourselves. Psychology, transcendental philosophy, science of consciousness etc. point towards a philosophical domain of subject matter. The question of the primordiality of the four viewpoints of destruction may not be torn out of the whole of the consideration. It is the question whether the objectivity character of the complex of lived experience is determined from these viewpoints or whether the problem of life in our formulation is in fact from the beginning posed in the direction of a domain of subject matter. With the opposition of the a priori problem and the problem of lived experience one has already reified. Where does this opposition between a priori and lived experience come from? From the two meanings of the word 'life'; their division was historically adopted; it is not primordial. Up till now there was the danger that we consider two problem groups and keep them in their division. If one, however, views this division itself as historically adopted, one is prevented from letting it be direction giving for all further decisions.

In our posing of problems up to now we have an inventory of real moments and contents; their combination determines the form of philosophy. With this the question about the actual facticity is forgotten if one conceives the areas of being from the perspective of transcendental philosophy. We have inventories as merely judged ones, as known ones, we have the task of the ultimate attainment of the individual from laws. However, we have neither an absolute consciousness nor an absolute facticity. The self in the actual enactment of life experience, the self in the experiencing of itself is the primal reality. Experience is not taking note but the vital being involved, the being worried so that the self is constantly co-determined by this worry. Environing world, with-world and self-world are no areas of being, not determined in something. All reality receives its primordial sense through the worry of the self. The manners of having and of pushing away the environing world hang together with the modification of the worry of the self. The worry of the self is a constant concern about the lapsing from the origin. Wherever it artificially lives itself out in tasks, actual self-worldly Dasein is spoilt. The accumulation of tasks of culture regarding content gives the calming assurance that the worry is on the right way. However, as far as the devotion (to the cultural tasks) is enacted, the self-world can be set aside and remain. But the task of enactment remains and the worry is always on the way of falling-away and even justifying itself for that. (All philosophy of culture and history belongs there, as e.g. that of Spengler, the modern aspirations towards a metaphysics etc.) This meaningfulness of the enactment must worry us, and the destruction of this meaningfulness must be purely preserved and secured against collapsing into subject matter-ness. (Neither does it concern practical tasks of culture!)

Philosophy has the task of preserving the facticity of life and strengthening the facticity of Dasein. Philosophy as factical life experience requires a motive in which the worry about factical life experience itself remains. We call this philosophical *fundamental experience*. (That is the proving of this motive.) It is no special illumination but is possible in every concrete Dasein where the worry brings itself back to actual Dasein. In the turnaround of this renewal, it is directed towards the self-world and from there the entire conceptuality of philosophy is to be understood and determined. From there the primordial determination of philosophy itself receives its sense. The *rigour* of philosophy is more primordial than every scientific rigour. It is an explication which goes beyond every scientific rigour to raise the being worried in its constant renewal into the facticity of Dasein and to make actual Dasein ultimately insecure.

If this sense of the enactment and of the relation of philosophy is grasped, then tasks arise that are foreign to the dominant direction of life and dominant philosophy. It is peculiar how quickly such a tendency is hushed up.

The only one on the way to such a philosophy, without, however, seeing his way, is Jaspers (*Psychology of Worldviews*, 1919). It is only possible on the basis of Diltheyian intuitions.

It is the task of phenomenology to put itself into that tendency towards the actual primordial Dasein and to always from anew throw the torch into all subject matter-systematic philosophy.

Appendix

1 On §§ 1–3

Every 'beginning' in philosophy is very promising, sweeping, but at first vacuous.

Task: to attain the idea of philosophy itself and access.

Motives for the pressing forward of 'life' as basic aspect: concrete formation of the sciences of history and the human sciences, their penetration of all life domains; formation of biology – development – sociology – psychology – Lotze – neo-Kantianism – psychology of lived experience; life philosophy – aesthetic studies – philosophy of culture – ethical (value) studies (fundamentally also in an aesthetic way, suspending statements and *existence*).

No philosophy of mediation:

between	philosophy as strict science and worldview philosophy
between	absolute validity – a priori and historical relativity
between	rationalism and irrationalism

but rather to reject the divisions in general as un-genuine and long since rootless and not radically motivated – grown together and interspersed with all sorts of motives.

It concerns the attainment of the concept of phenomenological philosophy. From the latter itself it will come to light that this concept cannot be *defined* (in the manner of the marking off *of a domain of subject matter* according to classes). The access shall be attained by a phenomenology of intuition and expression. From the outside, this looks like a contradiction. Likewise, it will also become clear that formal contradictions do not obstruct. The starting point of our consideration is a survey of the present problem situation; not fortuitously, *no merely pedagogical measure* or because it is the *common practice* that one always first orientates oneself 'a bit historically'. *The first rough indication of a problem tension*. To grasp *problem situation* more concretely. *Life primal phenomenon*.

2 On § 3

Basic flaws of symbolics (Spengler)

1. Altogether formal; it does not see the genuine primal correlation – essence relationship between act and object.
2. Unexamined in the background the Kantian transcendental philosophy.
3. It overlooks the structures because in general: the entirely original, irreducible form of objectification, of world formation and accordingly also that of understanding, of going along and of being able to emulate. 'Predominance of art' – the philosophically free formless intuition is lacking. (Formally transcendentally, it is simply symbolism.)
4. Related to this is the fact that the 'objectivations' are merely in their togetherness in a culture looked at with regard to the fact that they are expression. The hierarchical and respectively different structures of those worlds, their *whole* and the precedence of the one or the other are completely concealed. Therefore, the religious is not at all seen in the least. The whole is merely the sum.
5. The emphasis on the idea of culture and the concealment of the person and of its ultimate being means a fundamental alienation which in general allows the entire symbolics itself to be implemented.
6. This fixation of the view on formally summative symbolics, which gives to cultures and their phenomena the character of the thingly, isolated juxtaposition of plants, conceals the view for the phenomenon of personal life, of community and communication, and – beyond historical and other conditionalities – for the mere standing before God, for the being absolute. (Here the rootlessness reveals itself again and again.)
7. Through the schema of symbols the view is from the beginning pushed away from the possibility of seeing even the pure content as

such – as subsisting, according to its sense, in a way that is unworried about the act [*aktunbekümmert*] and unbound to the act.
8. Cf. the mixing up of consideration of symbols and symbolics as 'innerly necessary and unconscious symbolics'. Here, symbolics is virtually reified into a real *process*. 'All symbolics comes from fear' (238); 'unconscious symbolics'. Is the latter a *factum brutum*? Or are phenomenal characters somehow included in *living experience*? Where does the sense of *symbolics* aim?
9. The consideration of symbols does not seek to know an absolute. What are the primal phenomena that one has to accept?
10. *The location of the genuine phenomena of symbols and expressions:* the 'boundedness to the body', but not identity with the body or embodiment, organization *of the spirit*. Also the different forms of space, of the boundedness to the body and of the corresponding expression are only varieties of body-ness, not of the spirit and its a prioric *worlds*, which have *their* sense and their subsisting reality – in which they live, which *they have*, which subsists – only in forms of expression that, however, are not the world itself. The belongingness to a certain culture and world form is only seemingly the ultimate if one starts from and stops at the idea of culture.

Problem of apprehending symbols as expression interpretation

- Niveau and level character of apprehending.
- The pre-apprehending and co-having of that *which* expresses.
- The (intuitive) having of *what is expressed*.
- Universal motivated [?] symbolics:
    I. an ultimate identical what, as idea or in some other way, as long as I remain in the schema-sphere
    II. a fundamental sense of expression itself (direction – *ex-tension*).

3 On § 5

The following characterization of the phenomenological destruction is necessarily deficient because the phenomena are not anything like determined or even brought out, in whose context it only becomes fully understandable.

Still entirely without references to it, the interpretation of the phenomenological destruction as word explanation could be corrected to the effect that to this word explaining belongs an in principle methodological horizon so that this word explanation is no blind uptake of meanings that one can fortuitously come across and a merely technical attachment of this to a pre-given word form. The danger certainly exists – it is not always and everywhere avoided in philosophy itself – of tearing 'words' out of the context, of being pre-given a meaning from there, of fulfilling it intuitively and addressing what presents itself there as absolute, even a priori givenness. These efforts are especially intense where philosophizing is measured against the ideal of strict scientific knowledge, against the character of certainty, validity, strictness and unambiguousness of the evidence of this. And here it easily looks as if destruction was actually related to securing a strict and unambiguously available conceptuality, and only to that.

However, still entirely independent of the decision about whether or not philosophizing, according to relation, is to be grasped as a form of theoretical-scientific knowledge of domains of subject matter, it already turns out in a rough understanding of what is particular to the meaning complexes that they are expressly related to objects and their apprehension. A genuine explanation of meaning therefore stands in the service of the apprehension of objects and will also have to take into account its respective basic direction and structure. Then also the taking up of 'mere word meanings' loses the character of fortuitousness and arbitrariness. The concrete situation in which the *taking up* enacts itself and that in which the meaning fulfils itself must be understood and philosophically also taken into account. The situation is to be characterized according to its full concrete contours, as far as this is required for the understanding of the meaning complexes. Those have the particular character that they refer to each other in themselves for a vital understanding from out of a concrete situation – and not in an artificially reified detachment of a meaning as something that is self-contained and determined – that therefore there is the possibility of tracing those pre-delineations and bringing them out. Every vitally understood meaning – enactment of the concrete situation in which the not necessarily theoretical objecthood which is expressed through the meaning becomes experienceable – carries within itself the direction towards primordial sense-complexes and makes their loosening up concretely possible.

These sense-immanent pre-delineations themselves in turn lead, as it were, no proper life and may not be conceived as relationships objectively at hand, as an independent dynamic of per se existing meanings, but the pre-delineations are motivated in a preconception that also determines the how of the pre-delineations. With respect to the phenomenon of the preconception that pervades the situations it can now be merely said that it may not be grasped as a theoretical proposition or as a theoretical-scientific determination of tasks and the like. A preconception can have such 'as a result' but it does not have to. (As phenomenon – sense totality – it encloses in itself moments of content, of relation and of enactment in a different counter motivation and elevation.)

Phenomenological destruction is, as tracing the pre-delineations, as understanding their sense-according motives, at the same time preconception disclosing. It goes backwards and does not yet see the final goal in the discovered preconception, the preconception itself rather points to the so-called 'fundamental experiences' and therewith into the proper sphere of the origin that every genuine philosophical problem can be directed back to, or vice versa, from where it must be decisively motivated.

The phenomenological destruction (and the 'word explanation' that is now hardly to be comprehended as externally as before) is in the radical carrying-out not only preconception disclosing and in the enactmental understanding drawing attention to the fundamental experiences and the origin that alone are to be considered philosophically, it is itself *bound to preconception*. In the historical sequence of situations of the presented (communicated) destruction, the preconceptions arise in the end, their bringing-out also lies within the *goal*. In the primordial genuine enactment of the destruction in question the preconceptions that are to be brought out are already, even though not yet fully explicated – this is exactly achieved by the carrying-out of the destruction – anticipated and beforehand secondarily destruction guiding. The anticipation itself enacts itself in primordial fundamental experiences – and primordial preconceptions motivated from there – of the one who is philosophizing. The extent to which factical life experience plays along (environing, with- and self-worldly) cannot be decreed in an a priori and world-historical way. Aiming at this would already be a misunderstanding and a falling-away from one's own situation. The preconception, motivated according to fundamental experience, of the one who is philosophizing guides the bringing-out of the preconceptions that secondarily direct the destruction and are actually *to be destructed*, the primordiality or non-primordiality of which can then be dijudicated.

Destruction is therefore no critical smashing and shattering but a directed deconstruction [*Abbau*]; and this not in a detached area of meanings but it pertains to – provided that the in fact not yet fully explicated complex of meaning, pre-delineation, situation, preconception and fundamental experience is understood – the factical life experience and life-world itself in its historical concretion. It does not only pertain to this but is also primordially motivated *there*; its *necessity* is understandable from there. From factical life experience – more exactly its existentiell primordiality – the necessity, the scope of the phenomenological destruction as well as the difficulty of its enactment becomes understandable. Herein its role is also based, which is positively meaningful for philosophizing, as an enactment stage of the primordially enactmentally understanding explication.

Destruction is therefore no fortuitous means, to be employed in isolation for itself, for more limited philosophical and pre-philosophical knowledge purposes, merely annexed, as it were, to philosophizing and dispensable from case to case, but rather it also belongs to its enactment once one has understood that philosophizing moves within the field of factical life experience. This statement seems to be empty; nowadays one will only push at an open door with this because one after all keeps oneself as free as possible from a bottomless speculation – also where 'metaphysics' is supposed to be resurrected again – and sticks to empirical experience. Also, nowadays there will be no need for the explicit statement that what philosophy has as its object also plays a role in the factical life experience, can be found in it and is not a matter for the curiosity of some academics. It is not clear why on the basis of such construction-free and life-serving subject matter-ness of philosophy the destruction should have a special function. However, it is neither stipulated yet whether the preceding statement, that philosophy moves within the field of factical life experience, is correctly interpreted by what has been said. That must indeed be contested with reference to the fact that the interpretation is guided by the usual, exclusively epistemological discussion, as it pertains to the theory of science, of the concept of philosophy. This interpretation favours the opinion that this statement was about the decision regarding the question about the empirical or non-empirical way of grounding philosophical 'propositions' or about the delimiting of philosophy's domain of subject matter that would have to remain within the reach of empirical experience. One gives an epistemological sense to the expression 'factical life experience' and to the statement a corresponding meaning which for epistemology is certainly empty. However, the positive interpretation of the thesis cannot be given now. The rejection of the discussed aberrations is, however,

APPENDIX

considering the thinking habits nowadays, already shown correctly, even if it is not yet at all grounded. This is only achieved by a wholly concrete explication of factical life experience. (Cf. lecture on 'Basic Problems of Phenomenology', Winter Semester 1919/20 – the character of meaningfulness.[1])

Now only a primordial character of factical life experience shall be indicated in order to prove the primordial necessity of phenomenological destruction and to impress from the beginning its specific difficulty that this is, in principle, never entirely to be overcome. This primordial character of factical life experience shall be designated as the *fading* of meaningfulness. What is experienced in factical life has the content-, relation- and enactment-according character of meaningfulness. The fading implies the transition of the experience (understood in the sense entirety, concretely existentielly) into the mode of non-primordiality where the genuineness of the enactment and of the renewal of the enactment drop out, the relations for their part wear themselves away to a not especially distinguished unworked-out [?] character of accessibility and of acceptance, of being-busy-with. The content that in this way is divested of the primordiality of its accompanying relation and enactment stands in an average 'interest' and is in this way available in the ambit of experience. With the distance from the origin, availability more and more approaches mere usability. Fading does not mean to say that the experienced disappears from memory, is forgotten or receives no more attention. On the contrary, the faded absorbs the entire interest and pulls this into alienation and non-primordiality. (Fading, availability, usability, falling-away as existentiell full concepts [*Vollbegriffe*]. Cf. the existentiell explication, which starts from here, of the enactmental genealogy of areas of being and concepts of being and their concrete pre-delineations of possibility.)

From this disintegrating and depraving fading, factical life experience is endangered in its primordiality and therefore mixed with faded content, relation and enactment. (Therein is based the particular mixed character of factical life, from out of which a number of phenomena – lying in different situations and sense-relationships – like boredom, emptiness, fleetingness, speed, restlessness, insecurity of life become understandable.) Also the sciences and arts and philosophy itself are affected by the fading. It is not merely that they only at the outset and in the initiating decision are not primordial; even where something primordial succeeds, the fading is at work in the factical time of the enactment so that scientific theories, propositions and concepts just like philosophical explicata (in the mode of usability) of the no longer primordially experienced are taken up, handed down and further developed. If philosophy has to be determined as primordially enactmentally understanding and attention-drawing explication of factical life experience, then this explication necessarily always starts with the destruction. It begins in the faded. And if the aim is directed towards the explication of the sense of philosophizing itself, then pre-given philosophy is also to be understood destructively.

The scope of destruction is not a priori; it would be a systematic aberration to proceed programmatically; it is in the concrete and proves its existentiell meaning there. Provided that one is philosophically genuinely worried there is no reason to cross the borders into world history. But even for the concrete scope it is unacceptable to now give empty assurances.

Furthermore, destruction seems to strive for something like negative philosophy. That is still the old viewpoint under which the whole is taken. The destruction has in itself such an enactmental structure and lability that *in* it as a whole the positive itself comes forward, without something now having to be made into an issue explicitly and anew in the counter-direction. Here there is as little 'negative' as there is positive. There stirs again and again the hidden consideration of subject matter and objectivity which is already disengaged with the sense and the starting point of the destruction.

To show how the destruction is not, for instance, like 'critique', something that comes afterwards, that it is rather what is actually closer to the primordial, but only by going through what is set apart. The demolition (the setting apart) is only the expression of finitude. Setting apart and destruction may not be juxtaposed and subordinated but are to be seen in an existing totality. Destruction does not have the sense of reaching the proper through its result. The proper [*Eigentliche*] is destruction itself and its facticity, i.e. the setting apart that persists with it. 'Worry' is no idle turning around itself but rather the fact that destruction is part of it exactly co-constitutes the sense of concretion.

To supersede the isolation of the destruction even more acutely, more exactly, not to allow such a comprehension to arise. Connection with the explication.

There is the danger of seeing the destruction merely in the service of the theoretical, of the 'meanings' as 'theoretical concepts' or primarily in this deduced manner in theoretically reinterpreted phenomena. 'Meaning' here must be grasped existentially (enactmentally) as moment of the existentiell explication, in factical experience.

Destruction is, therefore, not transition and preparation for theoretical cleanliness and conceptual determination for the purposes of knowledge or as 'clear' (rationalistic) illumination of 'residual attitudes' – rationalistically misinterpreted genuineness (cf. Husserl!).

Such misunderstandings have in no time crept in whenever one forgets existence.

The primordiality that arises and becomes accessible both from the destruction and with it! The 'essence' has nothing more to do with a priorically valid or generally or absolutely necessary, also not 'essential' for a certain theoretical point of domain of subject matter, but the existentielly decisive and what enactmentally (primarily determined in this way) 'belongs' to it.

The phenomenological destruction

'brought out' through the existentiell experiential preconception. Primordiality motivated in: 1. the historicality of every spiritual or life situation in general; 2. the necessary falling-away of all life occurrences, existentiell fading, existentiell confusion; the existentiell sense of equivocation, provided that the meaning is not understood in a theoretical-subject-matter-meaning way. The going back to the origin *in principium* and the historical as primordial and intensive.

Destruction and phenomenological explanation of meaning

'Pre-delineations'. Destruction and its explication; the setting out of the proper primordial phenomenological-philosophical enactment and origin reflection [*Ursprungsbesinnung*]; of the clarifying description and descriptive clarification. Provided that in philosophy scientific knowing predominates (certainty, univocity, strictness etc.), the destruction seems to be essentially related to this and its achievement as clarification of meaning qua meaning:

I. destruction in the communication and sequence of communication
II. destruction in the primordially attaining enactment.

In I., it is only in the communication that the preconception expresses itself and the origin becomes accessible, that the access is enacted. In II., the preconception is first attained out of the fundamental experience (ultimately out of vital existence) and through its vital carrying through of the enactment the destruction is undergone; it expresses itself existentielly in the enactment of the destruction. With the bringing-out and the expression the preconception runs once again the risk of the set apart; it is never simply to be adopted again but – because existence is 'advanced' – is again to be drawn from the new situation, a renewal according and enactmental immerging in and emerging from existence. In this the extent of factical life experience (environing, with- and self-world) that plays along can be different.

Phenomenological-critical destruction

Clarifying of meanings, pre-delineations, situations, directions, the disclosing preconception, motivated in fundamental experience; bound to preconception, therefore presupposition (of which kind, to be seen later).

Therefore destruction not secondarily but necessarily belonging to phenomenology. It would be premature to designate it already now in its full scope and extent.

Indicating in the character of meaningfulness as such in environing, with- and self-world and in that it can fade, distances itself even more from the relation of existence.

4 On § 8 (p. 46 f.)

We have already made some concrete steps in a critical-phenomenological destruction. We have already said that it was bound to preconception, that therefore the direction in which it moves is motivated from a fundamental thesis and that this fundamental thesis itself is based on a fundamental experience, in fact on a phenomenological fundamental experience, so that the entire philosophical problematic intensifies towards the evidence of this fundamental experience and its genuine origin-character.

Insofar as we ourselves follow a destruction, concretely undergo it, we are pressed towards the *decisive fundamental experience* itself. Provided that it is of such a kind that it has itself in its enactment, there lies in it the primordial character of experiencing and intuiting and at the same time with this the essential articulation, the pre-delineations for how far it expresses itself and is to express itself. Therewith the concept of philosophy is determined, more exactly the *question* whether it can at all be determined differently than in the way that with and in the *achieved determination* only the repetition of the destructive regress is renewed [?] [...].[1]

(In this manner the primordial sense of 'having' and 'being' is attained, not the most general or formal, but the *phenomenological* one.)

5 On § 8 (p. 48 f.)

In the history of philosophy it is not that the pure disclosure of a new problem horizon asserts itself at the expense of the suppression of others, all the more if a new reorganization in parts and at times is continually effective.

Aristotle (psychology – biology), Descartes (cogito – rational metaphysics), Kant (transcendental problematic), the present (critique of psychologism, pure logic (theory of relations undecided, unarticulated [?]), psychology).

The explicit singling out of moments of enactment in general must encounter strong reservations, even more so if the claim arises that therein lies the centre of the philosophical problematic. The spreading of philosophy to empirical observation of facts and establishing of facts. Aiming at factically empirical occurring.

That such an attempt – departing from the present thinking habits – is exposed to abundant misunderstandings should not be surprising; it would also be futile to remove them straight away from the start. Everything spiritual requires the *enactmental appropriation*. Philosophizing – as I understand its task – is only entitled *to draw attention*, with all strictness, not, to be precise, in the concept- and thought-according object determination with regard to the individual sciences but with the *strictness* that is pre-delineated by the task and the goal of the drawing attention.

If this annoys you and you become irritated about the presented nonsense, enough has been already achieved. No revelations about the absolute are pronounced here. In order to later become aware of the scope of including the moments of enactment, it must be taken into account on what occasion we are led towards this.

APPENDIX

6 On § 9

Philosophy does not have a section, a precinct of the world as its object but rather it aims at the whole, namely in the way of rational knowing. In this way, it becomes understandable that in the course of its development primordial philosophical disciplines have separated and became individual sciences.

And one could expect that in the *unforeseeability of the cultural process* the development arrives at the point where philosophy will have dissolved into individual scientific disciplines. Nowadays, one seeks to revolt against this consequence, first by saying that then a problem sphere would still remain for philosophy, namely to ask how those sciences are possible, how they constitute themselves in consciousness. (But it is not foreseeable how also the whole of this problematic should not be able to become a self-contained science. Or one makes of philosophy an observation of types about the connection between the systems. Dilthey is also commonly dismissed with the catch word historicism.) Or else one seeks to avoid this process of disintegration by turning back to speculative consideration and metaphysics. The rise of a new metaphysics is nowadays the philosophical talk of the town. One thinks highly of philosophy for once more finding the courage for metaphysics. And one must at least already dream of a metaphysics and say that one does it if one does not want to run the risk of being regarded as backward in the company of philosophers.

In the background, one has a certain cultural belief that will never concede the possibility that philosophy is only seemingly a necessary good of mankind and that philosophy has the task of making itself look ridiculous with all rigour and of annihilating itself and furthermore of preventing itself from ever reoccurring.

7 On § 10 a

Phenomenological dijudication. Measure never an absolute one, relative above all if one considers that with this we strive [not only] towards the origin in general as idea but towards the concrete, the singular. Relativism unavoidable!

One has to give up the vocation again just as one got used to it. (Special task to investigate this fading of the theoretical argumentation and from there the encroaching on a reified philosophy.)

The most complete standpoint philosophy! Maybe standpoint philosophy can only be overcome by seeing the unavoidable position, the indispensable one, whereas the indispensability does not present itself in this way and guarantees that it exists on the basis of having to avoid a contradiction so that the theoretical-objective law of contradiction would after all be the ultimately grounding one.

The standpoint that every standpoint philosophy most often overlooks.

8 On § 12

Destruction: 1. no bringing-in of an alien standpoint and criticizing from there, 2. no merely immanent critique (logical consistency, completeness). The guiding tendency is immanently sought and likewise the explicating preconception. Pursuit according to the three directions of sense; this formal indication may not become an a prioric schema. This means a leap out of the origin and the manner in which this indication is itself motivated.

Phenomenological destruction always leads into positive questions; in the present case of the Natorpian position, the question about the right and sense or genesis of the origin and the origin meaning of the *formal*, then the problem of the connection between formal indication and theoretical attitude as well as the connection between the formal indication and the a priori.

Therefore a thorough understanding of the *entire* position and its *system unity* is indispensible. The presentation is such that for the destruction, as it were, that which is to be considered simply needs to be explicitly brought into relief. In the entire destruction, also of the remaining positions, it becomes apparent how we go along in the general tendency itself, first organically, then we ask whether it genuinely comes to a bearing and whether it is sufficient, i.e. is genuinely guided or whether the old (a priori) goal is not dragged along which one does not dare to tackle, which one at the most denies sceptically from the outside, but in this way after all remains at the same level.

The critical destruction is entirely misunderstood if it is construed as a reckoning in the last act of which the new then begins as my own philosophy – I do not need my own philosophy and therefore do not search for one but merely pose myself the task of drawing attention to the fact that we always strive for it [?] or not, that we however do not need it. [From the transcript of Oskar Becker: We do not philosophize in order to show that we need a philosophy but exactly in order to show that we do not need any.]

APPENDIX

9 On § 13

It lies in the sense of the phenomenological destruction that the sense-complex under discussion is apprehended as concretely as possible. Provided that the proper consideration of the origin matters to us, also the Natorpian position cannot be regarded merely according to a certain direction that maybe in one aspect is a very important one.

Where the consideration departs from questions specifically pertaining to the theory of science in order to advance from there to the fundamental experiences, it suggests itself to approach the question of the relation of apprehension from the next given side, from the question of the description (with regard to psychology).

In the course of last semester's lecture course the limitedness of this consideration became evident; the result of this is that the questions have to be posed more fundamentally. When working it out in an objective direction an inner discontinuity becomes apparent in this lecture, an [im-][1]balance that continues into the vacillation in terminology. It is necessary not to cover over this discontinuity and attempt un-genuine mediations and forceful interpretations. The details may have a limited value of appropriation, but only when they are genuinely comprehended. The 'argumentations' with respect to the description and its possibility are not quite amiss but incomplete.

By way of contrast, it would not be possible to say: In the method the natural-scientific-mathematical attitude is the predominant one and therefore the philosophical problematic is oriented in a one-sided way and is to be rejected. It is about matter of factly looking into the question and thinking about a motivation [?] and the structure of the guiding preconception in order to apprehend the *negation*, which also is to be attained in the destruction, as *positive motive of understanding*.

10 On § 14

The destruction totality is unitarily pervaded, not divided; in Natorp through the thought of the method, more exactly its *primacy*. The kind of arrangement of the questions and their answer is rooted therein. The primacy of the method is the ultimately determining feature of this position or it is itself only an expression of an underlying motive, of the actual preconception.

In order to understand this itself, the whole of this position must be

APPENDIX

kept in view. For the time being the aspect under the control of the primacy of the method serves us in this.

11 On § 15

Idea of constitution as it is; motivated in the *problem of knowledge*, radicalization of the task of securing, attitude. Nothing escapes this systematics. If one has devoted oneself to this preconception then every describing or getting caught by certain concrete individual questions appears to be un-philosophical, to be not at all philosophical, because it forgets to ask in return about the 'I' and to become aware of the fact that in the background the 'I' stands as precondition of the sense, of the ought and of doing.

We ask[1] what one does if one dedicates oneself to this preconception and what one attains if one is able to constantly and everywhere point back to this precondition and in this way systematically grounds a system.

The system manages to bring back to life what is dead, not for those who live but for those who are dead, those who dared the suicide of existence in order to attain in turn the life of thinking.

One is stunned if the system 'remains absent', if one is only served up fragments and obscurities and incompetence, even as philosophy. One raises a lot of philosophical clamour if one suddenly discovers that philosophy is unable to become systematized.

*

Description: Natorp – Husserl

[Transcript: Oskar Becker]

Description is destruction, immobilization of the life stream, objectification. Because through the description the infinite constitution complex is interrupted, the correlativity of consciousness is disturbed. Natorp's critique of the description is therefore justified from the constitutive viewpoint, but it remains to be seen whether it still makes sense in as much as one does not take it for granted.

Also in phenomenology, the concept of description is still determined merely negatively, it is delimited from the natural-scientific observation of causality and from the genetic observation of consciousness. Also here there is the danger of reifying consciousness, of dissolving it into thought-things and relationship connections, whereas the correlativity then feigns vitality.

12 On § 15 b

The idea of constitution is taken seriously. The question of enactment despite all universality of the above idea not alien and from the outside, provided that it asks in return about the motive of constitution, of securing. How does the idea and structure of the task and carrying-out present itself with regard to this motive and this tendency? Constitution: order complex. At the same time the justifiable, genuinely motivated sense inventory must let itself be determined on the basis of the idea of constitution itself in order to arrive at a philosophical decision about it.

The problem situation is at the same time such that with it itself the enactmental phenomenon must determine itself. The first position leads to the question whether the enactment itself is predetermined and can be delimited according to domains of subject matter. The decision prepares itself methodologically in the manner that one order determination sets itself against another. The complex of problems is then based on the question whether philosophy is a theoretical attitude and completes itself in its radical elaboration or already with the attitudinalness loses the primordiality.

13 On § 15 c

The underlying driving motive is the 'problem of the a priori', the formation in philosophy and its history. It is the central task to attain a radical posing of problems and a decision about whether the problem is at all genuinely posed:

I. The problem has nowadays (respectively in the course of the nineteenth century) attained for us a special form and new tension, namely through *historical consciousness*. What is at the basis of this? Is there not the danger that it – based phenomenally on what, based on which especially highlighted [?] experiences or *distinctions* – is itself made absolute? In the background an *evaluation*, namely the exclusive absoluteness of *culture*. In addition the transcendental and culture philosophy only a special philosophical expression: religion as cultural value. The sense-complexes are moved, by means of a

previous, however, as such naively enacted forcefulness, into this aspect, which makes absolute and is made absolute. The starting interpretation and dominance of the idea of symbol and expression is only an ultimate exponent. (In this exactly the fundamental reversal of the phenomenon of expression is to be shown.)
II. Since Kant and in the strong after-effect of neo-Kantianism of different denominations the a priori has been linked with the problem of consciousness and of the 'I'.
III. Linked with the logical relation: genus (generalities) – individual case.

Factical life experience is hidden from the object area of philosophy in a quite particular way just because it is not meaningful in its area character and the objects are not meaningful in the area complex, but in the structural form of factical life which is its primordial one.

In factical life, the sense-relations are not experienced in phenomenological contemporaneity but *lived* as ? – well, not as norms and laws to which something keeps to, neither as ideas that are strived for, nor as a priori which is individualized, but *lived in the enactment of factical life in personal existence and existence of the community*. The relation of the area, as immanent relation to the sense of personal existence, is essential, not contingent; expression [?], not a blurred generality into which it is made in certain theoretization – analogously with the 'at first' of experience or with the 'proper' of the a-theoretical. This 'reality' of the philosopher in factical life experience – the primordial one and modified according to the typology (pureness, highlighted-ness, distinguished-ness of the latter itself) in certain qualitative directions. (Immanent genuine transcendence of the primal factical.)

The primordial category for this being, its unity and manifoldness, is to be understood from life experience, personal existence and *meaningfulness*, situation. From there philosophy is to be understood as specific act direction, bearing and fundamental experience, and from *both* the essence of the philosophical 'concept' – of *concept formation* – [of the] *phenomenon of expression* is to be understood.

The *function of drawing attention – from out of* personal existence and *for* it – is co-determining for the structure of the concept.

The objecthood of philosophy does not have the subject matter-like theoretical character but that of *meaningfulness*, however of the *absolute one – primal-factical one*, related to personal existence as such, not to this

APPENDIX

and that historical bonded servitude in the factical concrete now here. In how far is the sense-genesis of knowledge as concrete logic of a domain of subject matter not sufficient for the construction and the ground laying of philosophy? It is not quite sufficient as it is rather an over-determination, over-determination as a bringing into the purely theoretical posture. As something less? That would be amiss – let us go into detail! Fundamental experience of existence, of which world?

14 On § 16

On the section about Dilthey

Constitution is ultimately a concept of order; in *Natorp*, where it is conceived radically logically, most acutely visible, but also where the panlogism is lessened, nothing is changed about the fundamental sense of the idea, not even if one, in light of this idea, seeks to possibly immediately make consciousness accessible to oneself. Therefore: life philosophically definitely determined as entirety of lived experience in an order complex.

Provided that philosophy strives for: bringing-out, securing, stabilization of Dasein, it has to be attempted to let the concept of philosophy be radically determined out of this motive, i.e. to pose the problem of lived experience in such a way that it genuinely corresponds to this motive.

To understand possibilities of posing the problems: now Natorp as sharpest opposition against Dilthey, the idea of constitution then probably forced back. To check how far it was successful, how far other motives determine the problematic, how far they are philosophically explicated at all and how far there is clarity about the sense of such explications. Dilthey, the 'life philosopher' – one is in grave danger of immediately starting with the most arbitrary misinterpretation and of giving up all positive new moments and tendencies and their understanding.

It is a still unsolved riddle of all spiritual interpretation that, when its motives and preconceptions are primordially experienced, explicitly appropriated and undergone, it proves its opening and revealing power. Maybe every philosophy can be determined according to the primordiality of the motives of interpretation and preconceptions of interpretation. (Constitution is a theoretically attitudinal and reifyingly order-like form of interpretation.)

APPENDIX

Concept of order and order complex, order determinations – nothing set apart, self-primordial, but in processes of elaboration and of *attitudinal* standing out.

Editor's afterword to the second edition

Volume 59 of the Martin Heidegger *Gesamtausgabe* contains the first publication of the lecture notes for the summer semester 1920 at the University of Freiburg. Heidegger lectured twice a week, that is '2-hourly' as one says. As the transcript from F.-J. Brecht documents, Heidegger began lecturing on 6 May and finished on 26 July 1920. On the last day he lectured twice. Those two lecture hours correspond to § 18 and § 19 of the present edition.

The entire manuscript consists of a 34-page lecture course manuscript and 40 appendices in four folders. For the transcription of the original manuscript, I had at my disposal a very good, however not gapless, typewritten copy by Fritz Heidegger and, as far as the lecture course manuscript is concerned, a complete copy from Dr Hartmut Tietjen. Apart from those, three handwritten transcripts of the lecture course by Oskar Becker, Franz Joseph Brecht and Karl Löwith were helpful. All available texts – original manuscript, copies and transcripts – were collated several times.

The 34 folio pages in oblong format show the well-known layout: the running text of the first draft on the left, marked insertions and unmarked additions on the right. In the last case, the placement within the entire text could only be determined from the height of the text, context or context of meaning. For this not infrequent case, the transcripts proved to be very important if they did not already make possible a direct determination of the location. If the placement was impossible in any of the mentioned ways, I moved the addition to the end of the paragraph and distinguished it from the running text by means of brackets.

EDITOR'S AFTERWORD TO THE SECOND EDITION

All headings except the ones of the main parts are mine; they were, however, chosen by closely following the text of the lecture course manuscript or that of the transcripts. In the manuscript, directly above the title of the lecture there is the note: 'Investigation of the concept of phenomenological philosophy – First Investigation'. This note is not mentioned in the transcripts and remains absent in the edition.

The division of the paragraphs is Heidegger's own. In a few cases, e.g. within larger insertions, a further subdivision was advisable. The punctuation often had to be added and differentiated since Heidegger for the most part only uses dashes within the paragraphs. All the quotations were verified; changes in the way of quoting made for the sake of the lecture presentation were undone again. From time to time the quotations had to be somewhat expanded in order to provide the appropriate relations for the insertions and additions.

The page references to the lecture course manuscript which can be found in the appendices do not allow any exact assignment because one page in the manuscript corresponds on average to four pages in the edited text. Appendices consisting of excerpts were not edited.

The extant course manuscript is not complete. Above all the part that was presented on Dilthey is missing. My search at the Deutsche Literaturarchiv in Marbach, in which I was aided by Dr Joachim W. Storck, remained unsuccessful. I therefore decided to complete the rest of the lecture course with the corresponding sections from Oskar Becker's transcript. The decisive factor in the choice of this transcript instead of the one of F.-J. Brecht or that of Karl Löwith was its greater completeness as well as its greater fluency. A transcription of F.-J. Brecht's virtually illegible transcript made by Dr Friedrich Hogemann at the Hegel-Archiv was very useful for me. Dr Hogemann kindly made it available to me with the permission of Professor O. Pöggeler, for which I express my gratitude to both gentlemen.

The transcript by Oskar Becker comprises 183 pages in small octavo format. It was taken on completely from page 112 onwards and also without any intervention with regard to the arrangement of the paragraphs (in the preceding printed text p. 113 ff.)

*

The importance that Heidegger obviously attached to this lecture course is expressed in the already mentioned title note 'Investigation of the concept of phenomenological philosophy – First Investigation'. It

EDITOR'S AFTERWORD TO THE SECOND EDITION

may, of course, be assumed that the all too obvious, however probably originally intended association with Husserl's *Logical Investigations* was the cause for dropping this relation again. Nevertheless this tentatively noted superordinate title captures very well the intention of the lecture course so that one can really say that this lecture course has a key role. More intensively than in any of the preceding and following lecture courses the new core of the phenomenological method, namely the phenomenological destruction which in turn leads into a phenomenological dijudication, is presented and treated upon. Some of it was adopted in the review of Jaspers (*Gesamtausgabe* vol. 9, p. 1 ff.).

The retained lecture title is to be understood from the preceding lecture course 'Grundprobleme der Phänomenologie' in which science in general was determined as expression complex of life and phenomenology in particular as origin-science of life per se (cf. *Grundprobleme der Phänomenologie* [1919/20], ed. Hans-Helmuth Gander, *Gesamtausgabe* vol. 58, p. 78 ff.). The part of the title 'Phenomenology of Expression' therefore relates to the particular character of phenomenological concepts, that is to be concepts of expression and not concepts of order (loc cit., p. 143, 240, 262). The part of the title 'Phenomenology of Intuition' refers in turn to that through which these concepts are formed, namely the phenomenological understanding, which is as understanding of the origin an 'intuiting preconception and reconception – in the sense of process-like *going-along-with*' (loc cit., p. 185).

It can not, therefore, be surprising that this lecture course played a considerable role in the astonishingly early reception of Heidegger in Japan (cf. *Aus einem Gespräch von der Sprache* [*Gesamtausgabe* vol. 12, p. 86]).

*

For the entrustment with the great responsibility, however also insight granting task of this lecture course edition, I remain gratefully beholden to Dr Hermann Heidegger.

Professor Dr Friedrich-Wilhelm von Herrmann and Dr Hartmut Tietjen kindly offered to collate the edited text once again. For this additional effort and the valuable editing assistance provided, I express my deep gratitude.

Finally, in the proofreading Andreas Preußner, MA, and Georg Scherer provided thorough and highly responsible assistance.

Claudius Strube
Cologne, May 1993

Glossary

area	*Bereich*
blocking-off	*Abriegelung*
bringing-out	*Hebung*
carrying-out	*Durchführung*
circumstantial	*zuständlich*
complex	*Zusammenhang*
complex of lived experience	*Erlebniszusammenhang*
concept formation	*Begriffsbildung*
conjunction	*Verbindung*
connection	*Zusammenhang*
conscious-ness	*Bewußtheit*
context	*Zusammenhang*
domain	*Gebiet*
domain of subject matter	*Sachgebiet*
enactment	*Vollzug*
enactmental	*vollzugsmäßig*
enactmental complex	*Vollzugszusammenhang*
environing world	*Umwelt*
epistemic	*erkenntnismäßig*
epistemological	*erkenntnistheoretisch*
existentiell	*existenziell*
experience	*Erfahrung*
experiencing	*Erleben*
fact	*Tatsache*
factical life experience	*faktische Lebenserfahrung*
facticity	*Faktizität*
factual	*tatsächlich*
factuality	*Tatsächlichkeit*

GLOSSARY

fade	*verblassen*
falling-away	*Abfall*
formal indication	*formale Anzeige*
human sciences	*Geisteswissenschaften*
immobilization	*Stillstellung*
indicate	*anzeigen*
intellectual history	*Geistesgeschichte*
lapse	*Abgleiten*
life-world	*Lebenswelt*
lived experience	*Erlebnis*
living experience	*Erleben*
meaningfulness	*Bedeutsamkeit*
mental	*seelisch*
object	*Gegenstand*
objecthood	*Gegenständlichkeit*
objectification	*Objektivierung*
objectivation	*Objektivation*
preconception	*Vorgriff*
pre-given	*vorgegeben*
pre-delineation	*Vorzeichnung*
primordial	*ursprünglich*
problem situation	*Problemlage*
relation	*Bezug*
relationship	*Beziehung*
self-world	*Selbstwelt*
sense-complex	*Sinnzusammenhang*
sense of content	*Gehaltssinn*
sense of enactment	*Vollzugssinn*
sense of relation	*Bezugssinn*
spiritual	*geistig*
subjectification	*Subjektivierung*
supersession	*Aufhebung*
supra-temporal	*überzeitlich*
temporality	*Zeitlichkeit*
validity	*Geltung*
viewpoint	*Gesichtspunkt*
vitality	*Lebendigkeit*
with-world	*Mitwelt*
worry	*Bekümmerung*

Notes

Introduction

§ 2

1   Thus, one strives for an a priori transcendental science of reason and of values as a distribution of the ultimate principles, values, goals of the factical life of the individual, of the community, of cultures in general.

§ 4

1   [German edition: *Zeit und Freiheit. Eine Abhandlung über die unmittelbaren Bewußtseinstatsachen*, Jena 1911.]
2   Cf. p. 28 ff. below
3   On the basis of which existentiell basic motive?'

§ 5

1   Whether we did not too hastily go astray in this after all, whether this formal phenomenology is something that we do not accommodate and, guided by Husserl himself, interpret in the sense of a science of reason. Perhaps the primordially proper sense is a justifiable one and has a supersede-able function in the concept of phenomenological philosophy. One of the deficiencies of fixed ultimate orientation becomes apparent in these fluctuations.
2   'Primarily' dialectical function – 'concepts of access'. Understandable

NOTES

   from existence relation and calling-attention-to. [*Ver. aus Ex. u. Afm.*]
3 Hans Diersch, 'Zur Lehre von der Induktion'. Sitzungsberichte der Heidelberger Akademie der Wissenschaften. Phil.-hist. Kl. Jahrgang 1915. 11. Abhandlung. Heidelberg 1915.
4 Nikolai Hartmann, 'Philosophische Grundfragen der Biologie' Göttingen 1912.
5 Primordially understandable from existence relation – factical life – calling attention to [*Afm.*].
6 Phenomena that have nothing at all to do with *space* but rather constitute a quite specific primordial sense-complex of factical life experience.
7 Availability, usability; concepts of reality and of being; existentiell genealogy of areas of being and concepts of being.
8 The whole of life, culture and so forth as 'utterance' of existence!
9 Cf. later where it becomes questionable whether this group division itself is to be maintained and not rather destructed. (On the destruction of the problem of the a priori.)

Part One

§ 6

1 A preconception was ultimately guiding, with regard to the existence relation and this preconception genuinely phenomenologically expresses itself in carrying-out the destruction – and therefore everywhere; not otherwise!
2 Cf. A. v. Harnack, 'Der Geist der Morgenländischen Kirche'. Sitzungsprotokolle der Preuß. Akademie der Wissenschaften, philosophisch-historische Klasse, 1913. p. 159 ('the experienced inner history' – his history; 'spirit of the people' – 'fate').

§ 7

1 [Cf. p. 63.]

§ 9

1 Cf. Wilhelm Dilthey, 'Das Wesen der Philosophie'. First published in: *Systematische Philosophie* (Collection: *Die Kultur der Gegenwart*), 1907; also in: W. Dilthey, G. S. Vol. V, p. 339 ff.

2 Cf. Heinrich Rickert, *Der Gegenstand der Erkenntnis*, 3. edition Tübingen 1915, p. 446 f.
3 Loc. cit. p. 442.
4 Heinrich Rickert, *Die Grenzen der naturwissenschaftlichen Begriffsbildung*. Tübingen, 2. edition 1913, p. 620.
5 Loc. cit. p. 621.
6 Georg Simmel, *Lebensanschauung*. München/Leipzig 1918, p. 38.
7 Ibid.
8 Loc. cit. p. 39.
9 Loc. cit. p. 97 f.

Part Two

§ 11

1 Relation of apprehension directed towards living experiencing itself!

§ 13

1 Paul Natorp, *Philosophie. Ihr Problem und ihre Probleme. Einführung in den kritischen Idealismus*. Göttingen 1911, p. 141.
2 Paul Natorp, *Allgemeine Psychologie nach kritischer Methode, Erstes Buch: Objekt und Methode der Psychologie*. Tübingen 1912, p. 128.
3 Loc. cit. p. 240.
4 The calling attention [*Afm.*] to non-existing!!
5 Loc. cit. p. 109.
6 Loc. cit. p. 69.
7 Loc. cit. p. 71.
8 Loc. cit. p. 125.
9 Ibid.
10 Ibid.
11 Loc. cit. p. 92 f.
12 Loc. cit. p. 126.
13 Paul Natorp, 'Bruno Bauchs "Immanuel Kant"' und die Fortbildung des Systems des Kritischen Idealismus', in: *Kantstudien* XXII (1918), esp. p. 448.
14 P. Natorp, *Allgemeine Psychologie*, p. 95.
15 Loc. cit. p. 190: 'immobilization'.
16 Loc. cit. p. 134.
17 P. Natorp, 'Bruno Bauchs "Immanuel Kant"', loc. cit. p. 432.

NOTES

18 Ibid.
19 Loc. cit. p. 433.
20 Ibid.
21 P. Natorp, *Allgemeine Psychologie*, p. 220.
22 Loc. cit. p. 195.
23 Loc. cit. p. 197.
24 Loc. cit. p. 198.
25 Ibid.
26 Loc. cit. p. 199.
27 Loc. cit. p. 229.
28 Loc. cit. p. 233.
29 Ibid.
30 Ibid.
31 Loc. cit. p. 237.
32 Loc. cit. p. 241.
33 Ibid.
34 Loc. cit. p. 243.
35 Loc. cit. p. 242.
36 Loc. cit. p. 243.
37 Ibid.
38 Loc. cit. p. 244.
39 Loc. cit. p. 245.
40 Ibid.
41 Loc. cit. p. 247.
42 Lower and upper limit (before all community, above all; monad of monads, unity of unities).
43 Cf. ibid.
44 Cf. loc. cit. p. 248.

§ 14

1 P. Natorp, 'Bruno Bauchs "Immanuel Kant"', loc. cit. p. 454.
2 Loc. cit. p. 440.
3 Loc. cit. p. 432.
4 Ibid.
5 Ibid.
6 P. Natorp, *Allgemeine Psychologie*, p. 239.
7 P. Natorp, 'Bruno Bauchs "Immanuel Kant"', loc. cit. p. 459.
8 Loc. cit. p. 448.

9   Ibid.
10 Bruno Bauch quoted loc. cit. p. 448.
11 Ibid.
12 Loc. cit. p. 449.
13 Ibid.
14 Loc. cit. p. 448.
15 Loc. cit. p. 432.
16 Ibid.
17 Loc. cit. p. 428.
18 Ibid.
19 Loc. cit. p. 429.
20 Ibid.
21 Loc. cit. p. 453 f.
22 Loc. cit. p. 454.
23 Ibid.
24 Ibid.
25 Loc. cit. p. 455.
26 Ibid.
27 Loc. cit. p. 431.
28 Cf. P. Natorp, *Allgemeine Psychologie*, p. 260.
29 Loc. cit. p. 32.
30 Loc. cit. p. 29.
31 Loc. cit. p. 30.
32 Ibid.
33 Loc. cit. p. 245.
34 Loc. cit. p. 27.
35 Loc. cit. p. 40 f.
36 Loc. cit. p. 41.
37 Loc. cit. p. 43.
38 Loc. cit. p. 48.
39 Loc. cit. p. 49.
40 Loc. cit. p. 50.
41 Ibid.
42 Loc. cit. p. 51.
43 Loc. cit. p. 59.

§15

1   [Cf. § 14 endnote 38.]

NOTES

2   'Origin', 'primordiality' with regard to the constitution, to unity thinking in the unity of the lawfulness of object determination.

3   Positive characterization of the *experience relation* designated by *description*.

§ 16

1   Cf. Natorp, *Allgemeine Psychologie*, p. 52.

2   Editor's comment: Probably a hearing or spelling mistake by Oskar Becker. The title is: *Die Einbildungskraft des Dichters*.

§ 17

1   Cf. Wilhelm Dilthey, 'Studien zur Grundlegung der Geisteswissenschaften.' Sitzungsberichte der Königlich Preußischen Akademie der Wissenschaften. Jahrgang 1905. Berlin 1905. p. 322–43. Here p. 326.

Appendix

3 On § 5

1   Editor's comment: *Gesamtausgabe* Vol. 58, edited by Hans-Helmuth Gander. Frankfurt a. M. 1993.

4 On § 8 (p. 46 f.)

1   [One word unreadable.]

9 On § 13

1   [Conjecture by editor.]

11 On §15

1   Pressing towards *decision*.

Index

absolute, the 14, 15, 19, 94, 96, 105, 110, 117, 138, 145
aesthetics 22, 69, 80, 131
Aristotle 8, 70, 75, 145
attitudinal complex 39, 40, 47, 48, 49, 58, 60
Augustine 75

being 6, 13, 35, 39, 41, 45, 49, 50, 51, 65, 80, 81, 84, 85, 87, 91, 106, 107, 127, 132
Bergson, Henri 10, 11, 19, 53, 63
Breysig, Kurt 11

Christian philosophy 8, 72, 75, 76
Christianity 15, 75, 76
concept 5, 19, 129
concept formation 1–5, 25, 130, 151
concern 101, 133
consciousness 18, 19, 73, 75, 82, 85, 86, 91, 94–107, 111, 114, 116, 117, 120, 121, 122, 123
constitution 99–114, 117, 126, 127, 129, 130, 150, 152

continuism 11
correlativity 80, 81, 84, 90, 94, 105, 110, 121, 149
culture 10–15, 40, 53, 60, 80, 81, 108, 109, 118, 125, 133

deconstruction 25, 139
Descartes, René 8, 74, 75, 130, 145
destruction 8, 21–9, 33, 51, 56, 57, 63, 70, 72, 73, 74, 76, 87, 90, 101, 113, 114, 125, 126, 130, 131, 132, 133, 137–44, 147, 148
dialectic 4, 16, 18, 19, 20, 105, 110, 112, 117, 128
dijudication 56–66, 73, 99, 101, 146
Dilthey, Wilhelm 9, 10, 11, 76, 114, 115–33, 146, 152

effective complex 121, 123, 126, 127, 128, 129
Enlightenment, the 8, 15
environing world 44, 45, 46, 62,

63, 64, 65, 113, 114, 116, 117, 132, 133
epistemology 52, 70, 128, 140
ethics 22, 69, 80, 131
existence 25, 27, 40, 47, 49, 57, 59, 61, 62, 63, 65, 66, 69, 72, 91, 93, 96, 101, 105, 143, 144, 149
experience 18, 24, 25, 26, 46, 58, 59, 70, 71, 74, 76, 77, 78, 83, 98, 101, 131, 133
expression 5, 11, 13, 129, 131, 136

factical life experience 6, 9, 26–8, 34, 35, 36, 38, 41, 42, 65, 71, 133, 139, 140, 141, 142, 144, 151
facticity 46, 49, 69, 121, 132, 133, 142
fading 26, 27, 141, 142, 143, 146
falling-away 22, 64, 106, 110, 133, 139, 141, 143
Fichte, Johann Gottlieb 75, 76, 92
formal indication 21, 47, 65, 77, 132, 147

genuineness 21, 26, 47, 141
givenness 24, 62, 102, 138
God 75, 94, 99, 109, 110, 136
Goethe, Johann Wolfgang von 122, 123
Greek philosophy 8, 72, 75, 84

Hegel, Georg Wilhelm Friedrich 12, 19, 20, 75, 76, 123
historical consciousness 8, 14, 15, 17, 150
history 3, 6, 7, 9, 15, 16, 21, 33–66, 128
Hölderlin, Friedrich 123

human sciences 2, 8, 9, 10, 12, 60, 118, 119, 120, 121, 124, 127
Humboldt, Alexander von 123
Husserl, Edmund 10, 22, 23, 81, 116, 125, 143, 149

'I' 18, 48, 73, 75, 86, 87, 90, 94, 95–9, 100, 101–6, 110, 114, 116, 126, 127
idea 14, 16, 50, 51, 53, 54, 55, 77
idealism 94, 108, 109
immobilization 19, 149
induction 26
intentionality 103
intuition 5, 124, 131, 133, 136

James, William 10, 76, 113, 114, 126, 127
Jesus 15, 38

Kant, Immanuel 2, 10, 18, 52, 75, 81, 90, 91, 92, 109, 120, 127

Lamprecht, Karl 11
Lask, Emil 3
life 8, 10, 11, 12–21, 28, 29, 53, 54, 108, 112, 113, 116, 119, 121, 127, 128, 129
life philosophy 8, 11, 12, 119, 126, 127
life-world 44, 117, 140
Lipps, Theodor 81, 106
logic 16, 19, 22, 52, 69, 70, 80, 81, 90, 92, 93, 94, 99, 110, 112, 117, 131
Logical Investigations (Husserl) 23, 125
Luther, Martin 58, 59, 75

Marburg school 10, 52, 88, 110, 112
meaningfulness 26, 44, 45, 62, 63, 64, 65, 124, 133, 141, 144, 151
metaphysics 15, 53, 133, 140, 146
Middle Ages, the 39, 74, 75
Munich phenomenology 22

Natorp, Paul 73–114, 115, 117, 118, 129, 130, 149, 152
natural science 33, 51, 78, 120
nature 113, 116, 121, 125
Neo-Kantianism 52, 120, 122, 135, 151
norm 9, 10, 51, 54, 56, 66, 69, 100, 116, 120, 121, 151
Novalis 123

objecthood 5, 7, 10, 14, 16, 17, 29, 69, 124, 151
objectification 48, 53, 72, 77–84, 85, 86, 90, 91, 92, 93, 94, 102, 104, 105, 106, 129, 149
objectivation 10, 11, 14, 39, 136
ought 10, 52, 53, 77, 80, 81, 84, 85, 87, 91, 92, 106, 107, 149

phenomenological basic posture 4, 6, 22, 23, 25, 26, 131
phenomenology 4, 5, 6, 20, 21, 22, 23, 24, 60, 77, 85, 86, 129, 131, 133, 136, 144, 149
Plato 8, 14, 16, 54, 70, 75, 94, 101, 117
poets 119, 120
potency 83, 84, 85, 86, 91, 105
preconception 24–6, 29, 54, 64, 69, 70, 74, 76, 85, 89, 99, 100, 101, 104, 106, 107, 110, 111, 122, 125, 128, 139, 140, 143, 144, 147, 149
pre-delineation 25, 27, 28, 29, 34, 37, 38, 71, 138, 139, 140, 143, 144
primordiality 27, 64, 65, 104, 111, 113, 114, 117, 118, 128, 132, 139, 140, 141, 143, 150, 152
psychologism 49, 125, 127, 145
psychology 9, 10, 23, 52, 69, 71, 72, 77, 81, 82, 83, 84, 85, 86, 90, 95, 99, 100, 101, 105, 106, 116, 121, 124, 125, 128, 129, 132
Psychology of Worldviews (Jaspers) 7, 20, 133

reality 39, 53, 77, 127, 128, 130, 132, 133
reason 10, 13, 14, 15, 16, 17, 23, 28, 51, 69, 92, 108, 109, 120, 131
reconstruction 76, 77, 82, 88, 104, 124, 129
reflection 3, 4, 71, 93, 118, 120, 124
religion 2, 13, 15, 20, 22, 75, 80, 109, 120, 131, 150
renewal 26, 57, 58, 59, 60, 61, 62, 63, 64, 65, 66, 114, 117, 133, 141, 144
Rickert, Heinrich 10, 52, 120, 126, 127

Scheler, Max 23, 53, 122
Schleiermacher, Friedrich 15, 123
science 2, 5, 6, 7, 9, 10, 13, 15, 22, 23, 27, 29, 33, 34, 35, 36, 38, 39, 40, 41, 51, 58, 61, 71, 74, 78, 80, 81, 108, 109, 112, 115, 118, 130, 141, 145, 146, 148

sense-complex 26, 33, 37, 38, 45, 46, 49, 51, 52, 55, 56, 57, 61, 66, 70, 71, 87, 100, 138, 150
Simmel, Georg 10, 12, 53, 56
Spengler, Oswald 11, 12, 14, 19, 20, 101, 121, 133, 136
subjectification 77, 79, 81, 82, 84, 86, 90, 91, 92, 105, 106, 129
supra-temporal 14, 15, 16, 55, 94, 114, 116
symbolics 11, 12, 20, 136, 137
system 2, 3, 6, 10, 14, 16, 18, 20, 29, 45, 56, 83, 91, 92, 107, 118, 127, 133, 149

temporality 15, 55, 116
theology 8, 15, 60, 72, 74, 75
tradition 3, 21, 33, 35, 36, 37, 39, 44, 45, 61, 62, 108, 109
transcendence 53, 151

transcendental 2, 3, 4, 10, 16, 18, 20, 22, 23, 82, 89, 90, 92, 97, 119, 120, 126, 127, 130, 132, 136

validity 9, 10, 13–16, 17, 18, 19, 20, 28, 33, 51, 52, 53, 57, 59, 80, 92, 108, 112, 138
value 7, 9, 10, 14, 15, 16, 28, 51, 52, 53, 54, 69, 77, 118, 120, 121, 123, 124, 127
vitality 16, 84, 87, 94, 100, 105, 108, 150

Windelband, Wilhelm 52, 75, 120
with-world 7, 44, 45, 46, 62, 63, 65, 108, 132
worldview 6, 7, 8, 28, 56, 71, 120, 130, 131
worry 109, 110, 131, 132, 133, 142

www.ingramcontent.com/pod-product-compliance
Lightning Source LLC
Chambersburg PA
CBHW050140240426
43673CB00043B/1738